Collins

English

Year 6 English

SATs Targeted Practice Workbook

Age 10 – 11

Year 6

SATs Targeted Practice Workbook

Shelagh Moore

Contents

Starter Test 4

Reading – Word Reading

Prefixes 12

Suffixes... 14

Adding Prefixes or Suffixes to Root Words 16

Root Words 18

Synonyms 20

Antonyms 22

Reading – Comprehension

Prose Genres.. 24

Formal and Informal Writing 26

Types of Poetry 30

Retrieving Information 34

Comparing Texts... 36

Progress Test 1 40

Writing – Transcription and Spelling

Prefixes..44

Suffixes..46

Homophones 48

Common Misspellings... 52

Possessive Apostrophes... 54

Silent Letters 56

One-off Spellings... 58

Using a Dictionary 60

Using a Thesaurus... 62

Progress Test 2...64

Contents

Writing – Composition

Audience and Purpose 68

Learning from Other Writers.......................................70

Settings, Character and Plot 72

Organising Your Writing 76

Précis 80

Proofreading 82

Progress Test 3..84

Writing – Vocabulary, Grammar and Punctuation

Verbs 88

Adverbs 92

Modal Verbs 94

Noun Phrases 96

Sentences 98

Relative Clauses 100

Commas 102

Hyphens, Dashes and Brackets.................................104

Semicolons, Colons and Bullet Points.......................106

Progress Test 4 108

Answers and Progress Test Charts 113

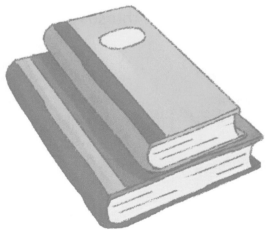

Starter Test

GP **1.** Rewrite these sentences, putting in the full stops and capital letters.

a) the midday bus from southsea will arrive in london in the evening

The midday bus from Southsea will arrive in London in the evening.

b) my name is daisy and my birthday is in may

My name is Daisy and my birthday is in may.

c) friday is the day of the week named after the norse goddess freya

Friday is the day of the week named after the norse goddess freya.

d) i was given an apple computer for my birthday

I was given an apple computer for my birthday.

e) dr adam smith met and married aida in new york

DR adam Smith met and married aida in new york

5 marks

GP **2.** Circle the words that should begin with capital letters.

andrew   morning   thursday   coin

finland   cooking   act 4   mars

5 marks

4

3. Make the following words into plurals.

a) box _boxes_

b) cow _cows_

c) calf _calves_

d) mouse _mice_

e) woman _women_

f) hippopotamus _hippos_

g) maid of honour _maids of honour_

h) sheep _sheeps_

i) penny _pennies_

j) hero _heros_

10 marks

4. Insert the conjunction that fits each sentence best.

when	if	because	although	either...or

a) _When_ my brother comes with us _either..or_ I go home with him!

b) We will be able to move _when_ the crossing opens.

c) I will leave soon _because_ I don't want to be late for tea and upset my mother.

d) We can clear the table _if_ you can make some space in the sink for washing the dishes.

e) Yasmeen wanted to see the film _although_ she thought the monster might be frightening!

5 marks

PS 5. Insert the punctuation and correct the spelling mistakes in the following passage. Write it out in the lines below.

> grace was a kind girl, she often shared her lunh time snack with her friends as they liked the cakes her mother baked for her graces mother was a chef and worked in the nearb hotel makeing wonderful meels for the gests

Grace was a kind girl, she often shared her lunchtime snack with her friends, as they liked the cakes her mother baked for her. Grace's mother was a chef and worked at the nearby hotel, making wonderful meals for the guests.

12 marks

6. Write out the following sentences, putting speech marks in the correct places.

a) Hi there, said Colin. Are you going to the park?

"Hi there," said Colin. "Are you going to the park?"

b) Mandy cried out, Look out! There's a car coming!

Mandy cried out, "look out! there's a car. coming!"

c) Are you all right? asked the police officer, I have the number of the car – that was very dangerous driving!

"Are you all right?" asked the police officer, "I have the number of the car – that was very dangerous driving!"

d) Mandy and Colin managed to reply, We're OK thanks.

Mandy and Colin managed to reply We're ok ook thanks

4 marks

7. Put the correct pronoun in each sentence.

she	they	who	yours	themselves	us

a) _She they_ thought they could manage to make the cake

   by _themselves_.

b) The girl looked hard and _She_ saw the boy running towards her.

c) "_who_ are you?" asked the teacher.

d) Shall we take my car or _yours_?

e) The guides left _us_ when we arrived at our destination.

5 marks

Starter Test

GS **8.** Insert the correct **prefix** at the beginning of the words in the sentences.

    a) The teacher did not expect the children to _____ obey him.

    b) They did not usually _____ behave.

    c) He waited _____ patiently until they settled down.

    d) "You can _____ write your stories in your best writing," he told them.

    e) Freya had already written her _____ biography so she had a lot to rewrite!

5 marks

GS **9.** Insert the correct **suffix** at the end of the words in the sentences.

    a) He was asked to find the correct inform_____ for the history book.

    b) Sad_____ the holiday came to an end and the friends parted.

    c) We worked out the measure_____ for our new carpet.

    d) The annoying boy turned out to be quite like_____.

    e) There are many friendly people in our neighbour_____.

5 marks

10. The letters in these words are jumbled up. Write the words correctly.

a) sadders   _____

b) ebleiev   _____

c) tcrenia   _____

d) papsidera   _____

e) xeperinece   _____

f) nguahyt   _____

g) accoinos   _____

h) ehigwt   _____

8 marks

11. Underline the correct word to complete the sentence.

a) She **accepted/excepted** the prize from the judge.

b) The children **break/broke** the lock and escaped from the wicked witch.

c) The bus **fare/fair** was very expensive.

d) The **not/knot** was tied tightly.

e) The **meet/meat** was cooked well and tasted good.

f) We **mist/missed** the start of the race but saw who was the winner.

6 marks

12. Read the passage and answer the questions. Answer in sentences using the information from the passage.

> Native fashion, they delayed their departure from one day to another till the first Rains caught them and the unmended roofs let in a flood, and the grazing-ground stood ankle deep, and all life came on with a rush after the heat of the summer. Then they waded out – men, women, and children – through the blinding hot rain of the morning, but turned naturally for one farewell look at their homes.
>
> They heard, as the last burdened family filed through the gate, a crash of falling beams and thatch behind the walls.

a) Who is leaving the village? _____

_____

b) What had caught them? _____

_____

c) What was unmended? _____

_____

d) How is the rain described? _____

_____

e) What did the families hear as they left? _____

_____

5 marks

13. Read the poster and answer the questions.

 Pantomime
Aladdin

Performances daily from December 18th 2014
until January 12th 2015.
Afternoon matinees Monday, Wednesday,
Friday and Saturday at 4 pm.
Daily evening performances at 7 pm.
No performances on Sunday.
Come to this amazing panto!
Laughs and excitement as Aladdin outwits
Abanazer – his wicked uncle!
Comfortable seats and inexpensive tickets
available if you book early!

a) What is the poster advertising? _____

b) On what day are there no performances? _____

c) On which days are there no afternoon performances? _____
_____

d) The poster contains facts and opinions. List three opinions given
in the poster. _____
_____
_____

e) Why is it advisable to book early?
_____

5 marks

Marks........ /80

11

Prefixes

Challenge 1

GS **1** Put the correct prefix at the beginning of the word to change the meaning of the word. Draw a line from the new word to the new meaning.

| dis | in | inter | re |

a) _____city   to cease to be visible, to vanish

b) _____audible   not loud enough to be heard

c) _____appear   to do again

d) _____take   a fast rail service between towns

8 marks

Marks.......... /8

Challenge 2

GS **1** Put the correct prefix in front of the word to change the meaning of the sentence.

a) He was _____known to the police.

b) They were known to always _____behave.

c) The dogs _____patiently waited for their dinner.

d) At times her writing was _____legible.

4 marks

2 Insert the correct word in the sentences.

| unlock   semi-retired   refurnish   relearn |

a) I need to _____ the information if I am to pass the test at my second attempt.

Prefixes

b) The thieves stole all our furniture and we had to

_____ the house.

c) I had to _____ the door to let myself into the house.

d) My Gran is _____, which means she sometimes works and sometimes has a lot of free time.

4 marks

Marks.......... /8

Challenge 3

1 Insert prefixes in the passage so that it makes sense. Use each prefix only once.

(**mis**)   (**re**)   (**no**)   (**un**)   (**in**)

The boy walked along the dusty, _____pleasant road. He was

looking for somewhere to hide. He wanted to be _____visible

to those following him. He arrived at a shallow ford. The

water trickled over stones and along to a waterfall. The boy

thought he would _____lead his followers. He left tracks on

the other side of the ford and _____traced his steps. He hid

behind the waterfall. The people trying to find him crossed the

ford and were soon _____where to be seen.

5 marks

Marks.......... /5

Total marks .... /21   How am I doing?

13

Suffixes

Challenge 1

GS | **1** Underline the suffix at the end of the word and draw a line to match it to the correct meaning.

dragged

transferring

sisterly

comfortable

teacher

| like a sister |

| a person whose occupation is teaching others |

| at ease, relaxing |

| pulled |

| moving a person or things from one place to another |

10 marks

Marks......... /10

Challenge 2

GS | **1** Add a suffix to the words so that the following sentences make sense. You may need to change the spelling of the root word before adding the suffix.

a) Her dog was sitting comfort_____ under the table.

b) His behaviour was consider_____ better today.

c) The teacher refer_____ the pupil to the Headteacher.

d) An explain_____ was difficult to understand.

e) Dracula is a horror_____ monster who has frightened many filmgoers.

5 marks

2 The following words all contain a suffix. Insert the correct word in the sentences.

| collision | preparation | visibly | substantial |

a) She was _____ shocked when she saw the birthday feast her friends had organised.

b) The _____ of the feast must have taken a lot of planning.

c) Her friends ate a _____ part of the feast.

d) When they were clearing up there was a _____ that meant the floor was covered in food!

4 marks

Marks.......... /9

Challenge 3

 1   The following words all contain a suffix. Place them correctly in the passage below.

| happiness   sitting   curious   wondering   patiently |

Once, a man was _____ _____ on

a chair in his kitchen. He was _____ what he

could have for his dinner. There was nothing in the cupboard.

Suddenly there was a knock at the door and in came his

daughter. She placed her basket on the table and began to

quickly empty it. Her father was _____. What was

in the basket? Food began to appear on the table. The man was

filled with _____ and thought that his daughter

was wonderful.

5 marks

Marks.......... /5

Total marks .... /24   How am I doing?

Adding Prefixes or Suffixes to Root Words

G Grammar   P Punctuation   S Spelling

Challenge 1

 1 Insert the correct prefixes and suffixes to make the root word make sense in the sentence.

a) The two child_____ were absent

from school and miss_____ the school trip.

b) It is danger_____ to ride a bike

without wear_____ a helmet.

c) The food was burnt, so it was _____possible to eat it.

d) Jake gave a great perfom_____ in the dancing competition.

e) Driving without pass_____ a test is _____legal.

f) A _____honest person is _____liked by those they lie to.

10 marks

Marks......... /10

Challenge 2

 1 Add a suffix to the root word to make a new word so that the sentence makes sense. You may need to change the spelling of the root word before adding the suffix.

a) You have to be observe_____ if you want to see a tiny insect on a leaf.

b) Washing your hands helps stop

infect_____ diseases from spreading.

c) His reason for being late was understand_____ as he had missed the bus.

Adding Prefixes or Suffixes to Root Words

d) Good writing is very satisfy_____ to read and gets better marks.

e) The chair was very comfort_____ to sit in while she was waiting.

5 marks

Marks.......... /5

Challenge 3

1 Draw a line to match the prefix to its meaning.

Word	Prefix	Prefix meaning
a) interchange	inter	many
b) autobiography	auto	hear
c) multipurpose	multi	outstanding
d) audition	audi	across
e) transport	trans	between, among
f) superman	super	self, own

6 marks

Marks.......... /6

Total marks .... /21   How am I doing?

Root Words

G Grammar   P Punctuation   S Spelling

Challenge 1

S **1** Here are some root words. Add a new beginning or ending to each one to make a new word. The first one has been done for you.

a) front becomes <u>con</u>front

b) myth becomes myth_____

c) cow becomes cow_____

d) bus becomes _____bus

e) fame becomes fam_____

f) vision becomes _____vision

5 marks

Marks.......... /5

Challenge 2

GS **1** Draw lines to match the 10 root words to make five new words.

Root word	Root word	New word
water	paper	_____
pea	works	_____
note	ever	_____
news	book	_____
for	nut	_____

5 marks

Marks.......... /5

Root Words

Challenge 3

1 Choose a compound word to insert into the sentence so that it makes sense.

| fishbowl | candlelight | newscaster |
| warm-blooded | stagehand |

a) The _____ read the news in a serious voice.

b) I was excited; being the _____ in the school play was an important job!

c) It must be quite boring just swimming

   in circles in a _____.

d) Reptiles are not _____ creatures, which is why they like to lie in the sun.

e) She had to perform her dance in the _____ as there was a power cut.

5 marks

2 Alter the words in the passage so that the passage makes sense by adding the correct beginning or ending to each root word. Remember that you might need to change the root word before adding an ending.

Walk_____ along the road, she arrived at the pond. She

was checking for _____poles. It was spring and she was

hope_____ to find some to take for the school pond. She

put some into a container and put it into her ruck_____.

On the way home she was over_____ by her friend.

He exam_____ her container and was _____pressed.

7 marks

Marks........./12

Total marks ..../22   How am I doing?

Synonyms

Challenge 1

GS 1 Circle the word that means the same or has a similar meaning to the word at the beginning of the line.

a) **affectionate**   unfriendly   difficult   caring   unkind

b) **big**   heavy   light   huge   round

c) **leave**   lead   gather   depart   forget

d) **walk**   talk   potter   stroll   run

e) **nice**   horrible   chatty   agreeable   unpleasant

5 marks

Marks.......... /5

Challenge 2

 G 1 Underline the synonym that fits the sentence best.

a) As he ran, the man **looked/gazed/spied** an opening in the fence that he could escape through.

b) She hurried home as it was late and the **dusk/sunset/ evening** was drawing in.

c) Mr Smith was told to **check/control/impede** his habit of biting his fingernails.

d) The cheeky kittens got up to all sorts of **mischief/ harm/roguery** when they were left at home by their owners.

e) Children of all ages are usually **content/ glad/delighted** to be given a treat for good behaviour!

5 marks

Marks.......... /5

Synonyms

Challenge 3

1 Replace the words underlined in these sentences with a synonym from the box below. Write the correct synonym so that the sentences make sense.

| usually | great | glanced | distinguished | declared |

a) "Children," <u>said</u> the teacher, "today we are going to behave perfectly." _____

b) The children <u>looked</u> at each other. _____

c) One child said, "But Miss, we are <u>normally</u> good." The teacher smiled and let them into a secret. _____

d) Today the school was having a <u>special</u> visitor and the best class would meet her. _____

e) The children made a <u>big</u> effort to behave and eventually met the visitor! _____

5 marks

Marks.......... /5

Total marks .... /15

How am I doing?

21

Antonyms

Challenge 1

S **1** Choose words from the box that are opposite in meaning to the ones listed.

expensive   decline   multiply   exit   worse

Word	Antonym
a) accept	_____
b) better	_____
c) cheap	_____
d) divide	_____
e) entrance	_____

5 marks

Marks.......... /5

Challenge 2

S **1** Read the sentences and write the antonyms of the words underlined in the spaces at the end of each line.

a) It was a <u>sunny</u> day. _____

b) The place on the bus for buggies was

<u>occupied</u>. _____

c) "We are at <u>war</u>!" replied the General. _____

d) The hall was <u>empty</u>; they had thought that no-one would

come to the concert. _____

e) The <u>friends</u> sat down to talk things through. _____

5 marks

Marks.......... /5

Antonyms

Challenge 3

1 Place the antonyms in their correct places in the sentences.

a) (big, little) The _____ girl was unable to reach the

_____ pot on the shelf.

b) (cold, hot) When it is _____ you should drink

_____ drinks.

c) (antique, young) He liked _____ shops even

though he was _____ and poor.

d) (filthy, shipshape) Ben's house was

_____ when he moved into

it but he soon had it _____ and tidy.

8 marks

2 Complete the sentence with a word that is an antonym of the one underlined.

a) When you take a test make sure you read the <u>question</u>

carefully before you select your _____.

b) Cinderella wore a <u>beautiful</u> dress to the ball, unlike the

_____ dresses her stepsisters wore.

c) "Did you _____ to go to the library or did you
<u>forget</u> again?" asked her father.

d) _____ people are liked but <u>rude</u> people are avoided.

e) Her dad drove an <u>expensive</u> car but she only could afford

a _____ one.

5 marks

Marks......... /13

Total marks .... /23   How am I doing?

23

Prose Genres

Challenge 1

1 Read the extract and complete the sentences using words from the passage.

> Mowgli, who had never known what real hunger meant, fell back on stale honey, three years old, scraped out of deserted rock-hives – honey black as a sloe, and dusty with dried sugar. He hunted, too, for deep boring grubs under the bark of the trees, and robbed the wasps of their new broods.

a) Mowgli had never known what _____

_____ _____.

b) The words describing the honey's colour are _____

_____ _____ _____.

c) Mowgli hunted for _____ _____

_____ under the bark of trees.

3 marks

Marks............/3

Challenge 2

1 Read the extract and answer the questions about it.

> I remember him as if it was yesterday, as he came plodding to the inn door, his sea-chest following behind him in a hand-barrow; a tall, strong, heavy, nut-brown man; his tarry pigtail falling over the shoulders of his soiled blue coat; his hands ragged and scarred, with black, broken nails; and the sabre cut across one cheek, a dirty, livid white.

a) What was following the man in a hand-barrow?

_____

b) How was the man walking to the door?

_____

c) What colour was his coat?

_____

d) What type of cut did he have?

_____

4 marks

Marks.......... /4

Challenge 3

1 These questions ask you to compare the extracts in Challenges 1 and 2. You may want to read them again.

Both are classic tales that tell us about a boy called Mowgli in the first story and a boy called Jim in the second.

a) Which boy is remembering his adventures using the first

person? _____

b) Which boy's story is told by the writer?

_____

c) What sort of situation is the first extract describing to us?

_____

d) What genre do these extracts come from? Circle the correct answer.

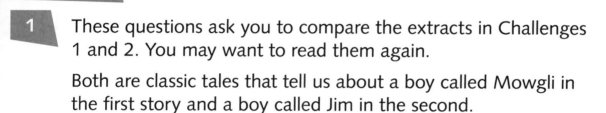

adventure   science fiction   fantasy

4 marks

Marks.......... /4

Total marks .... /11   How am I doing?

Formal and Informal Writing

1 Read the sentences and decide if the writing is **formal** or **informal**.

a) Dan's diary: I was really worried when I saw the lion but I didn't panic, I just got back into the car really slowly! _____

b) I am pleased to inform you that you have been selected for the football team. _____

c) Hi! I'm writing to let you know you're on the football team! _____

d) All the children are to receive a parcel when they arrive at the hostel. _____

4 marks

Marks.......... /4

1 Rewrite these informal sentences as formal sentences.

a) Hi there, we're going to have a blast at the beach!

_____

b) You'd better pack or you'll be late!

_____

c) He didn't want to leave the meeting, as he hadn't spoken yet.

_____

d) "Where's the treasure map, Cap'n?"

_____

4 marks

Marks.......... /4

Formal and Informal Writing

Challenge 3

1 Here are two extracts. Read them carefully and carry out the task.

Letter to parents

> Dear Parents
>
> …The provision of free school meals for KS1 is something that schools have to provide by law. Free school meals ensure that all children eat a healthy meal each day. Children need to eat properly if they are to be able to concentrate and learn. The school provides them with a well-balanced and nutritious meal that they appear to enjoy…
>
> Yours sincerely

Chat with parents

> Hello parents
>
> Welcome to our school. The kids in KS1 all get free school meals. We've got to provide them as it's the law. The kids need a well-balanced and nutritious plate of food. We'd like them to eat healthily. Anyway, they enjoy the grub we serve!

a) Are any contractions used in the letter to parents? _____

b) Are contractions used in the chat with parents? _____

c) Which piece uses slang? _____

d) What do both extracts tell the parents about the meals? _____

_____

e) Is the letter to parents formal or informal? _____

f) Is the chat with parents formal or informal? _____

6 marks

Marks.......... /6

Total marks .... /14   How am I doing?

Formal and Informal Writing

Challenge 1

1 Read the following recount from the Second World War.

My father was a sergeant major who fought in the Second World War. His unit finally ended up in Holland where he bought a Dutch dinner service to send to his fiancée in Scotland. He sent the plates for the dinner service one by one after wrapping them carefully in straw. When he ran out of straw he used stuffing from pillows in his tent. Soon the pillows became flatter but the dinner service arrived in Scotland without any breakages! The others in the tent never worked out why their pillows were flatter.

List five key facts in the story in the correct order. The first one has been done for you.

a) My father fought in the Second World War.

b) _____

c) _____

d) _____

e) _____

4 marks

Marks.......... /4

Challenge 2

1 Read the story below and then put the facts into order.

The Ghost of Jacob Marley visited his old friend Scrooge. He entered the house and found Scrooge in bed. It was midnight and Marley's Ghost had come to warn Scrooge about the possible consequences of his selfish and miserly way of living.

a) Who? _____

b) What? _____

c) Where? _____

d) When? _____

e) Why? _____

5 marks

Marks.......... /5

Formal and Informal Writing

Challenge 3

1 Read the diary extract and answer the questions.

> Today, I had a good day. My teacher actually said my work was good – I think he was ill! I got a credit point. I now have 9; only 1 more to go! That was in the morning. In the afternoon I left school early as I had to go to the dentist. Mum got a talking to about taking me out of class but I was happy. I was even happier when the check up showed I didn't need any fillings – great sighs of relief! At home, we had my favourite meal of jacket potato and beans AND A CHOCOLATE PUDDING!!! I did my homework and played with my Lego with dad. I'm writing this before I go to bed. What a great day! See you tomorrow diary!

a) Is the writing formal or informal? _____

b) What person is it written in? _____

c) Is it written mainly in the past or present tense?

_____

d) What feelings is the writer expressing – happy

or unhappy? _____

e) Why is the type of the pudding in capital letters?

_____

5 marks

Marks.......... /5

Total marks .... /14   How am I doing?

29

Types of Poetry

Challenge 1

1 Draw lines to match the poem types to their descriptions.

acrostic	A three-line poem with each line having a set number of syllables. It originated in Japan.
haiku	A poem with a word written vertically and each line of the poem beginning with a letter of the word.
limerick	A poem that makes no sense but can sound interesting or amusing.
nonsense	A poem without a regular rhyming pattern or regular verses which can use ideas in any order.
non-rhyming	A humorous poem of five lines with a special rhyming pattern.

5 marks

Marks.......... /5

Challenge 2

1 What sort of poems are the following?

a)

There was an old man with a beard
Who said, "It is just as I feared!
Four larks and a wren,
Two owls and a hen,
Have just built a nest in my beard!"

This is a _____ .

c)

An old silent pond…
A frog jumps into the pond,
Splash! Silence again.

This is a _____ .

b)

This Is Just To Say
I have eaten
the plums
that were in
the icebox
and which
you were probably
saving
for breakfast

Forgive me
they were delicious
so sweet
and so cold

This is a _____ .

3 marks

Marks.......... /3

Types of Poetry

 1 Here is an extract from a narrative poem. Read it carefully and answer the questions.

> Half a league, half a league,
> Half a league onward,
> All in the valley of Death
> Rode the six hundred.
> "Forward, the Light Brigade!
> Charge for the guns!" he said:
> Into the valley of Death
> Rode the six hundred.
>
> "Forward, the Light Brigade!"
> Was there a man dismayed?
> Not tho' the soldier knew
> Someone had blundered:
> Theirs not to make reply,
> Theirs not to reason why,
> Theirs but to do and die:
> Into the valley of Death
> Rode the six hundred.

a) What lines are repeated in each verse?

_____

b) What were the riders told to 'charge' for?

_____

c) Were the men dismayed at the order?

_____

d) What does the poet say that, as soldiers, they have to do?

_____

e) Which line tells you that the poet thought the 'Charge for the guns!' was a mistake?

_____

5 marks

Marks.......... /5

Total marks .... /13

How am I doing?

Types of Poetry

G Grammar   P Punctuation   S Spelling

Challenge 1

1 Match the definitions to the literary devices below.

metaphor   simile   alliteration   onomatopoeia

a) _____ is the use of the same sound at the beginning of each word.

b) A _____ is a direct comparison where one thing is said to be, or have the qualities of another.

c) _____ is when we use words to imitate sounds.

d) We use a _____ to compare two things by using the word 'like' or 'as'.

4 marks

Marks.......... /4

Challenge 2

1 Read the lines from the poems and identify what term fits the words or phrases in the following lines.

simile   metaphor   alliteration   onomatopoeia

a) 'Down, down, down,
Down to the depths of the sea' _____

b) 'And like a thunderbolt he falls' _____

c) 'All the world's a stage
And all the men and women merely players' _____

d) The ice groaned, creaked and cracked
The skater screamed
And that was that! _____

4 marks

Marks.......... /4

Types of Poetry

Challenge 3

1 Read this extract by Shakespeare and answer the questions.

> All the world's a stage,
> And all the men and women merely players;
> They have their exits and their entrances,
> And one man in his time plays many parts,
> His acts being seven ages. At first, the infant,
> Mewling and puking in the nurse's arms.
> Then the whining schoolboy, with his satchel
> And shining morning face, creeping like snail
> Unwillingly to school…

a) What is Shakespeare writing about? _____

_____

b) In the extract, what is 'a stage'? _____

_____

c) What is the infant doing? _____

_____

d) Does the schoolboy like going to school? _____

e) Write the simile that gives the answer to d). _____

_____

f) What is the name of the three dots at the end of the extract and what do they indicate?

_____

_____

7 marks

Marks.........../7

Total marks .... /15

How am I doing?

Retrieving Information

Challenge 1

1 Read the passage and answer the questions.

Sofia, Alex and her friend Malia were at the lake with Sofia's mum and dad and their dog Into. Into was a young Springer spaniel who seemed to like going into the lake to retrieve sticks. Alex thought Into was mad to do this as the water in the lake was very cold. Malia thought he might get cold so they decided to walk back to the house to dry him. Sofia's mum explained that Into was a breed of dog that liked going in water. Her dad took the view that he just liked being messy!

a) How many people were at the lake? _____

b) Who else was with them? _____

c) What was he? _____

d) What was Alex's opinion about Into's activity? _____

_____

e) What was Malia worried about? _____

_____

f) Was Sofia's dad giving a fact or opinion? _____

6 marks

Marks.......... /6

Challenge 2

1 Write whether the sentence is giving a fact or an opinion.

a) I think that you are feeling better today. _____

b) The girls tidied the classroom for the teacher. _____

c) It's going to rain today – look at those dark clouds. _____

d) Ten children did not hand in their homework this morning!

_____

4 marks

Marks.......... /4

1 Read the passage from *A Christmas Carol* and answer the questions using evidence from the passage.

> "A merry Christmas, uncle! God save you!" cried a cheerful voice. It was the voice of Scrooge's nephew, who came upon him so quickly that this was the first intimation he had of his approach.
>
> "Bah!" said Scrooge, "Humbug!"
>
> He had so heated himself with rapid walking in the fog and frost, this nephew of Scrooge's, that he was all in a glow; his face was ruddy and handsome; his eyes sparkled, and his breath smoked again.
>
> "Christmas a humbug, uncle!" said Scrooge's nephew. "You don't mean that, I am sure."
>
> "I do," said Scrooge. "Merry Christmas! What right have you to be merry? What reason have you to be merry? You're poor enough."

a) Pick out the words that show Scrooge's nephew is feeling happy. _____

b) How do we know from his response that Scrooge did not like Christmas? _____

c) How do you think the nephew felt after the walk that made him feel 'all in a glow'? _____

_____

d) Why did Scrooge think his nephew should not be merry?

_____

_____

 4 marks

Marks.......... /4

Total marks .... /14 How am I doing?

Comparing Texts

Challenge 1

1 Read the two narratives and answer the questions.

Extract A

There was a certain island in the sea, the only inhabitants of which were an old man, whose name was Prospero, and his daughter Miranda, a beautiful young lady. She came to this island so young, that she had no memory of having seen any human face other than her father's.

Extract B

Hello, you might be wondering who I am or what I am. Let me tell you. I am a dinosaur! I live in a world that is very different to yours. You might recognise some of the plants that I see every day but many would be strange to you. I live in a world of coniferous forests, groves of cycads and fern-like plants. Flowering plants like magnolia, holly, ginkgo, dogwood, horsetails and ferns make my world beautiful.

a) Is extract A a personal or impersonal account? _____

b) Is extract B a personal or impersonal account? _____

c) Which extract is written in the third person? _____

d) Is the language in A used to inform or describe? _____

 4 marks

Marks.......... /4

Challenge 2

G **1** Use the extracts in Challenge 1 to answer these questions.

a) Write down the noun that tells you who the narrator is in

extract B. _____

b) Which word describes Prospero? _____

c) Find a sentence or phrase in each extract that describes the setting.

Comparing Texts

A: _____

B: _____

4 marks

Marks.......... /4

Challenge 3

1 Read the extract and answer the questions.

Dog walker loses dogs!

Dan Smith, aged 22 years, employed as a dog walker in Cowplain, was involved in an incident earlier today. He was walking four dogs for clients. He suddenly ran to the aid of an elderly man who had collapsed in front of him. Dan called an ambulance. When he looked up his dogs had disappeared.

Dan searched the area and could not find them. As he retraced his steps he heard barking. His dogs were in a house near where the incident had occurred. Al Jones had taken them in when he saw they were loose. He wanted to keep them safe.

When Al was told the incident was over, he handed the dogs back. "It was a relief to find them safe," said Dan, "I just wish he had told me he was taking them!" The dogs were returned to their owners. The elderly man was discharged from hospital safe and well thanks to Dan's speedy help.

a) What type of text are you reading? _____

b) Who is the story about? _____

c) Where does the story take place? _____

d) When did the incident happen? _____

e) What happened? _____

5 marks

Marks.......... /5

Total marks .... /13

How am I doing?

37

Comparing Texts

Challenge 1

1 Read the poster and answer the questions.

> ## Sunshine Holidays 4 You!
> Would you like a beach holiday with your family?
> Are you looking for exciting places that you can afford?
> **Find summer sunshine, sand and sea in Wales**
> Send for our brochure; it will give you ideas of the best
> places for you and your family!
> www.TravelWales.com

a) What is the title of the poster? _____

b) What is the poster about? _____

c) What will you find in Wales? _____

d) What will the brochure tell you? _____

_____

4 marks

Marks.......... /4

Challenge 2

1 Read the diary extract and answer the questions.

> ### DIARY OF A LITTLE GIRL
> ### IN OLD NEW YORK
> ### (1849–1850)
>
> August 6, 1849
>
> I am ten years old today, and I am going to begin to keep a diary. My sister says it is a good plan and when I am old, and in a remembering mood, I can take out my diary and read about what I did when I was a little girl.
> I can remember as far back as when I was only four years old, but I was too young then to keep a diary, but I will begin mine by telling what I can recall of that far-away time.

Comparing Texts

> The first thing I remember is going with my sister in a sloop to visit my aunts, Mrs Dering and Mrs L'Hommedieu, on Shelter Island. We had to sleep two nights on the sloop, and had to wash in a tin basin, and the water felt gritty.

a) How old is the little girl? _____

b) Look at the style of writing. How can you tell it is not the diary of a modern girl? _____

c) What clue in the text tells you she is not writing things as they happen? _____

d) Is this writing information or recount writing? _____

4 marks

Marks.......... /4

Challenge 3

1 Read the following sentences and say what type of text they are.

| persuasive | descriptive | recounting | reporting |

a) I remember when I was a young child, I had to eat my greens. _____

b) The conclusion is that the pond must have a fence around it for the safety of the children. _____

c) "Please, let me try. I will be very careful," said Mira. _____

d) The food smelt delicious. There were green peas and yellow peppers set out around the chicken and rice. _____

e) When the lesson ended, the boys and girls quickly ran outside to play before their teacher changed her mind! _____

5 marks

Marks.......... /5

Total marks .... /13   How am I doing?

Progress Test 1

GS **1.** Read the sentences and put in the correct word by adding a prefix or suffix to the words below.

mercy	happy	cycles	arm	port

a) He had an _____ of dirty clothes for the wash.

b) Sophie was the _____ she had been for weeks, her father was coming home!

c) The _____ from school was good for a change and his parents were happy.

d) The king decided to forgive the thief as he wanted

   his people to think he was _____.

e) The cycle race was unusual as the cyclists rode

   _____ (three-wheeled cycles).

5 marks

GS **2.** Match the words to make compound words.

Root words	Root words	Compound words
high	metre	a) _____
flow	base	b) _____
land	light	c) _____
data	scape	d) _____
kilo	chart	e) _____

5 marks

3. Put in the word that makes best sense in the passage.

notice	interrupted	praised	disappeared
unruffled	newsreader	reading	

40

The newsreader was _____ the news when she

was _____ by an intruder. The masked person

held up a _____ which read 'Happy Christmas'.

He then _____ .

"I will now carry on _____ the news," said the

_____ presenter who was later _____

for keeping calm.

7 marks

4. Draw a line under the word that means the same as the word at the beginning of the line.

a) **crafty**   devious   nasty   thoughtful

b) **almost**   distant   apart   nearly

c) **hunger**   glutton   starvation   indigestion

d) **imitate**   act   alike   mimic

e) **vain**   proud   difficult   ugly

5 marks

5. Write the word that has the opposite meaning – the antonym.

| rough | liquid | destroy | hero | repair |

a) coward _____   b) smooth _____

c) break _____   d) build _____

e) solid _____

5 marks

6. Read the texts and answer the questions.

Text 1

The Eagle

He clasps the crag with crooked hands;
Close to the sun in lonely lands,
Ring'd with the azure world, he stands.

The wrinkled sea beneath him crawls;
He watches from his mountain walls,
And like a thunderbolt he falls.

Text 2

Animals as workers

In a circus animals are often trained to work or perform for humans. They can be made to jump through hoops, ride bikes or stand on large tubs if they are elephants. In times past ponies used to work in the pits hauling coal. Domestic animals, especially dogs, are trained as helpers to people so that they can lead their lives in their homes more easily. Guide dogs for the blind are a positive example of animal and human working together. It is generally thought that the dogs are well cared for and affectionate and hard working.

a) What does the Eagle clasp with crooked hands? _____

b) What colour is azure? Circle the correct answer.

bright blue   **pale green**   **purple**   **black**

c) What animals stand on large tubs? _____

d) What animals hauled coal? _____

e) Are the answers you have given facts or opinions? _____

f) How is the sea described in Text 1? _____

g) Write out the line that is the simile in the poem. _____

_____

h) Is the last sentence in the passage fact or opinion? _____

☐ 8 marks

7. Identify the formal and informal sentences.

a) Please identify yourself. _____

b) Hi, are you on holiday? _____

c) The guards reported to their commander that they had

completed their tasks. _____

d) Dear Diary, I've had an awful day today! _____

e) I'm going to work. Bye for now, see you later! _____

f) Smith, reporting for duty, sir. _____

☐ 6 marks

8. Read the following sentences and say if they are:

| descriptive | recounting | persuasive | reporting |

a) It would be good if we all helped each other as we would finish

sooner. _____

b) There were twenty people rescued from the sinking

ship. _____

c) I remember the storm was very fierce and we were very much

relieved when we were rescued. _____

d) The blue sky and sparkling sand made the day on the beach

appealing for the family. _____

☐ 4 marks

Marks........ /45

Prefixes

Challenge I

⟨GS⟩ **1** The prefixes below mean 'not'. Put the correct prefix in front of the words in the sentences.

☆ **in** ☆ **im** ☆ **ir** ☆ **il** ☆ **non** ☆ **anti**

a) He attended the meetings _____ frequently.

b) The doctor gave the patient the _____ dote in order to save his life.

c) After the accident the girl was _____ mobile.

d) The doctor's writing was _____ legible.

e) The painting that the thieves stole was _____ replaceable.

f) The woman was a _____ believer and did not want to join them.

6 marks

2 Draw a line from the prefix to the meaning.

Prefix	Meaning
auto	round
circ	two
tele	self
trans	far
mis	across
bi	wrong

6 marks

Marks.........../12

Prefixes

Challenge 2

1 Complete the sentences by inserting the correct word.

anticlockwise	transatlantic	infrequent
	bicycles	telescope

a) There are _____ flights to the South Pole so people need to book early.

b) How many _____ are available for the race?

c) We ran in an _____ direction around the playing field.

d) To view the stars you need more than a _____.

e) The first solo non-stop _____ flight in an aeroplane was by Charles Lindbergh in 1927.

 5 marks

Marks.......... /5

Challenge 3

1 Read the passage and insert the correct prefix so that it makes sense.

Amir was _____able to go to the party as he had stomach

ache. He was _____appointed as he had been looking

_____ward to the party. His friends did not forget him; they took a

piece of frozen birthday cake to his house. His mum _____frosted it

and Amir was able to enjoy a piece of cake when he had

_____covered. Amir thought his friends were _____replaceable.

 6 marks

Marks.......... /6

Total marks .... /23 How am I doing?

Suffixes

Challenge 1

 1 Add the correct suffix to the end of the word underlined so that it is spelt correctly and makes sense in the sentence. Rewrite the sentence.

a) The child was <u>worry</u> that his homework would be incorrect.

_____

_____

b) The scientist was an <u>observe</u> woman.

_____

_____

c) Her <u>assist</u> was not helpful at all.

_____

4 marks

d) He was <u>refer</u> to his boss when he arrived late again for work.

_____

_____

Marks.......... /4

Challenge 2

1 Using the words in the box, match the meaning with the correct suffix. Then write a word from the box that uses the suffix.

Meanings:	**full of** **to write** **action** **capable of being** **make or become**
Words:	**manage thankful magnify prescribe excitable**

Suffixes

Suffix	Meaning	Word
able	_____	_____
age	_____	_____
fy	_____	_____
ful	_____	_____
scribe	_____	_____

10 marks

Marks......... /10

Challenge 3

1 The words with suffixes are jumbled except for the first two letters. Write the words correctly.

a) The <u>decoranoit</u> of the bedroom went well and the children liked their new room. _____

b) The holiday-maker <u>suendn</u> herself by the pool.

_____

c) The children were <u>trvllaeing</u> to school when the driver got lost. _____

d) It was <u>polybsis</u> the best day of their lives when they won the cup. _____

e) "<u>Cairgn</u> for a loved one is a good thing to do," said the preacher. _____

5 marks

Marks......... /5

Total marks .... /19

How am I doing?

Homophones

G Grammar   P Punctuation   S Spelling

Challenge 1

S **1** Look at the words in bold in the sentence and underline the word that fits the sentence.

a) The bride walked down the **aisle/isle** on the arm of her father.

b) The children were **aloud/allowed** to talk after they had finished their work.

c) When Bella bought a new watch, she had to **alter/altar** it so that it was at the correct time.

d) Max ate the horrible-tasting **serial/cereal** for breakfast.

e) A **heard/herd** of wild elephants walked slowly past the lions resting under the tree.

5 marks

Marks.......... /5

Challenge 2

S **1** Choose the correct word to fit into the passage so that it makes sense.

peace	piece	picture	pitcher	sight	site
missed	mist	presence	presents	presents	practising

It was her birthday and Aimee received many _____. Her

friends were impressed by the _____ of the table laden

with tasty food. In the playroom, the clown was _____

for his performance after the birthday tea. Aimee was sad that

her best friend had _____ the party. She would send her

a _____ of the cake and save a _____ for her.

6 marks

48

Homophones

2 Circle the word that fits the meaning.

a) Goods stolen during riots: (lute) (loot)

b) A small dried seedless raisin: (current) (currant)

c) To give up or relinquish something: (wave) (waive)

d) The civic head of a town or city council: (mayor) (mare)

4 marks

Marks......... /10

Challenge 3

1 Match the correct pairs of homophones.

fair		son
ewe		pale
pail		fare
sun		there
their		you

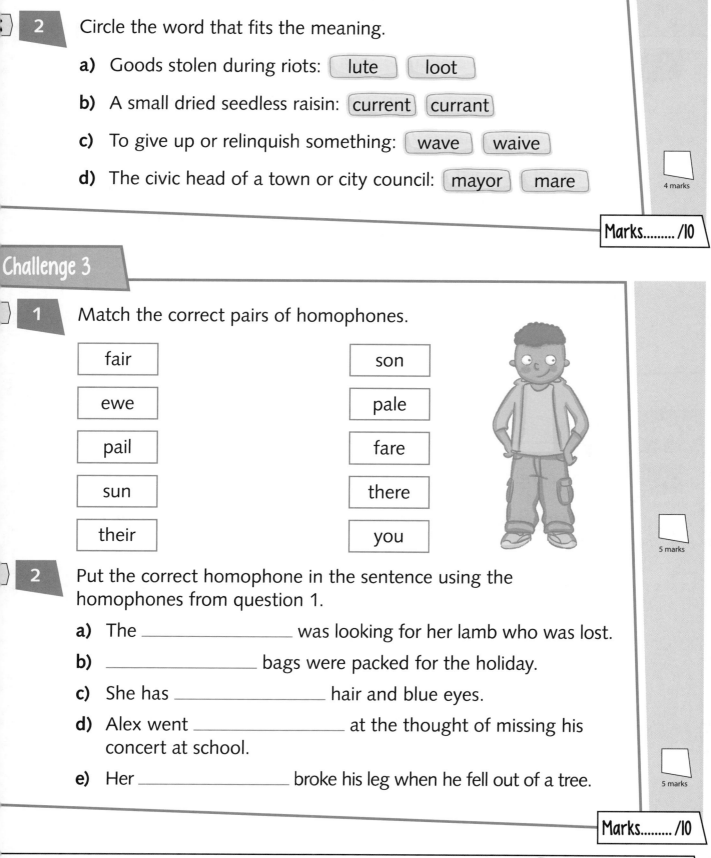

5 marks

2 Put the correct homophone in the sentence using the homophones from question 1.

a) The _____ was looking for her lamb who was lost.

b) _____ bags were packed for the holiday.

c) She has _____ hair and blue eyes.

d) Alex went _____ at the thought of missing his concert at school.

e) Her _____ broke his leg when he fell out of a tree.

5 marks

Marks......... /10

Total marks .... /25

How am I doing?

Homophones

 Grammar   P Punctuation   S Spelling

Challenge 1

S 1   Underline the correct word in each sentence.

a) The **steak/stake** was sharp and went into the ground easily.

b) "We will need **flower/flour** for the cake," said the cook.

c) The **waste/waist** had been dumped
in the park overnight.

d) We saw the girl **stare/stair** in disbelief at
the teacher when her mark was read out.

e) Monopoly is one of the most popular **bored/board** games,
especially for families.

5 marks

Marks.......... /5

Challenge 2

S 1   Put the correct homophone in the gaps in the sentences.

a) (bizarre, bazaar) When they visited the _____ they were

amazed at the _____
items for sale.

b) (band, banned) Hoppy's

_____ was

_____ from the show as they arrived late.

c) (steel, steal) The plan to _____ the

_____ models went wrong and the thieves were
arrested.

50

d) (bee, be) "I want to _____ dressed as a

_____ for the party!" exclaimed Mo.

e) (flaw, floor) When the builders had finished laying the

_____, they discovered a _____ in the

wood and had to start again.

5 marks

Marks.......... /5

Challenge 3

1 Correct the spelling of the underlined homophones in the sentences.

a) When he went to meet his <u>threfa</u>, he had to walk <u>fahtrre</u> than he expected.

_____ _____

b) The thief was <u>cuahgt</u> and taken to <u>outrc</u> for his trial.

_____ _____

c) He had to <u>pusea</u> to clean the dog's dirty <u>sawp</u>.

_____ _____

d) At the party the <u>tuegs</u> <u>edsesug</u> the correct answer to the puzzle.

_____ _____

e) <u>Wihhc</u> way did the <u>thiwc</u> go?

_____ _____

10 marks

Marks.......... /10

Total marks .... /20

How am I doing?

Common Misspellings

Challenge 1

  1

Underline the correct spelling in each group. If you underline the wrong one, remember you need to learn the correct British English spelling of the word, not the American version.

a) accomodate, acommodate, accommodate

b) begginning, beginning, begining

c) cemetry, cemetary, cemetery

d) disasterus, disasterous, disastrous

e) equipment, equippment, aquipment

f) forreign, foreign, foreigne

g) guaranty, guarantee, garentee

h) immediat, imediate, immediate

i) mischievous, mischievious, mischevous

j) neighbor, neghbour, neighbour

10 marks

Marks......... /10

Challenge 2

  1

Put the letters on the whiteboard in the spaces to spell the words correctly.

a) occ__s__on__l__y

b) parl__a__en__

c) q__e__e

d) rec__m__e__d

e) s__p__r__te

f) s__om__ch

6 marks

Marks.......... /6

52

Common Misspellings

Challenge 3

1 Correct the words in the poem so that it makes sense. Write the lines out correctly.

a) Eye have a spelling chequer,

_____

b) It came with my Pea Sea.

_____

c) It plane lee marks four my revue

_____

d) Miss Steaks I can knot sea.

_____

e) Eye strike the quays and type a whirred

_____

f) And weight four it two say

_____

g) Weather eye am write oar wrong

_____

h) It tells me straight a weigh.

_____

i) Eye ran this poem threw it,

_____

j) Your shore real glad two no.

_____

k) Its vary polished in its weigh.

_____

l) My chequer tolled me sew.

_____

12 marks

Marks.........../12

Total marks ..../28   How am I doing?

Possessive Apostrophes

 G Grammar   **P** Punctuation   **S** Spelling

Challenge 1

PS **1** Correctly write out the singular word that needs an apostrophe. The first one has been done for you.

a) Her fathers book.   <u>   father's   </u>

b) The workers tools.   _____

c) Bens castle.   _____

d) The teachers pencil case.   _____

e) Is this Lolas book?   _____

f) I'll run to Freds.   _____

5 marks

Marks.......... /5

Challenge 2

PS **1** Correctly write out the plural word that needs an apostrophe. The first one has been done for you.

a) The teams match was on Friday.   <u>   teams'   </u>

b) The birds nests were broken.   _____

c) The lawyers clerks charged a lot of money for their work.   _____

d) All the cats paws were dirty.   _____

e) "Are all the girls dresses ready for the dress rehearsal yet?"   _____

f) Blackbirds eggs look different to the ones that magpies lay.   _____

5 marks

Marks.......... /5

Possessive Apostrophes

Challenge 3

1 Insert the correct word, from the box below, in the passage using the apostrophe correctly.

| cleaners   Hatchs   teams   girls   Jakes   minutes   boys |

Jake's father was not pleased with him. _____

coat was covered in mud. "You'll have to get that cleaned at

_____ the dry cleaners," he said. Jake was upset.

The _____ team was going to the park to practise

for their match. Jake ran to the dry _____ shop

and then to the park. The teams were doing their stretches

before the game. Their _____ football was to be

used in the match.

The _____ team was also playing and they

needed a ball too. "Here you can have ours," said the

manager of another team. The girls began their match. It was

five _____ hard work before they scored a goal.

After the matches were over the teams compared notes. The

girls had won their match but the boys had only drawn theirs.

7 marks

Marks.........../7

Total marks .... /17   How am I doing?

Silent Letters

G Grammar   P Punctuation   S Spelling

Challenge 1

S **1** Some words have silent letters – hundreds of years ago they were sounded but not today. Underline the silent letter in the following words.

a) knee

b) plumber

c) island

d) lamb

e) solemn

5 marks

Marks.......... /5

Challenge 2

S **1** Read the sentence and fill in the missing silent letter to make the word correct.

a) The internet can be a good source for general
   __nowledge.

b) Tom Thum__ was a tiny person in a fairy tale.

c) The s__issors were good for cutting paper.

d) We__nesday is named after the Nordic God Woden.

e) I __racked my brains for the solution.

f) The dog __nawed at his bone.

g) "Do you know the ans__er?" the teacher asked.

h) The __nife was very sharp and cut the meat easily.

i) "Lis__en," whispered the poacher. "I hear the gamekeeper coming."

j) When you __rite, you should hold your pen correctly.

10 marks

Marks.......... /10

Silent Letters

Challenge 3

1 Underline the words in the following passage that contain silent letters.

> The ballet teacher was cross. Her class had not practised their dance. The corps de ballet were an important part of the performance. They would have to practise through the night despite being exhausted.

6 marks

2 The words with silent letters are scrambled. Write them correctly.

> The nogme crept into the clearing. He began to bmcil the tree. He hasnged his teeth when he saw the fairy queen. He had come to cause cahos and planned to werkc the celebrations.

a) _____

b) _____

c) _____

d) _____

e) _____

5 marks

Marks.......... /11

Total marks 26

How am I doing?

57

One-off Spellings

Challenge 1

S **1** Put the correct word in the space in the sentence.

to	two	too	there	their
they're	where	were	your	you're

a) Place the plates over _____ please.

b) _____ going to be late if you do not hurry.

c) You _____ can come _____ the party

_____ if you like.

d) _____ _____ they going for their holidays?

e) They think they have lost _____ luggage!

f) Do you think _____ going to stay now they

have found _____ luggage?

10 marks

Marks.......... /10

Challenge 2

S **1** Here are some jumbled spellings. Write out the words spelt correctly. The first two letters are correct.

a) michseif   _____

b) diseel   _____

c) sodleir   _____

d) sicenlyre   _____

e) supirres   _____

5 marks

One-off Spellings

2 Insert the missing letters then write the word correctly.

a) a_commodate _____

b) str_t_gy _____

c) mis_h_ _v_us _____

d) temp_ _ at_r_ _____

e) g_ar_ _tee _____

5 marks

Marks......... /10

Challenge 3

1 Underline the correct spelling.

a) The convict was **desparate/disperate/desperate** to escape.

b) The **symbel/symbol/cymbol** for oxygen is O.

c) Drummers must be able to keep the **rythm/rithem/rhythm** when they are drumming.

d) Sarah was the most useful **secretary/seceretary/secretery** the school ever had.

e) The toddler had a lot of toys to **ocupy/occuppy/occupy** herself and her **frends/freinds/friends**.

6 marks

Marks......... /6

Total marks .... /26

How am I doing?

59

Using a Dictionary

Challenge 1

1 Words that start with the same letter are put in alphabetical order using the first two or three letters. Put these words in alphabetical order.

accompany	communicate	accord	committee
	community	accommodate	

a) _____   b) _____

c) _____   d) _____

e) _____   f) _____

6 marks

Marks.......... /6

Challenge 2

1 Dictionaries use guide words at the top of a page to help you find words between them. Here are some guide words with their pages. Answer the questions.

briefcase 98 brink	evasion 286 everyone	jagged 450 jaw

presence 668 press	tailback 881 take away

a) On which page would you find the word 'take'? _____

b) The word 'evening' can be found on page _____.

c) Where would you find the word 'brilliant'? _____

d) What would you spread on your toast that is on page 450?

_____

e) Would you find the word 'presenter' on page 668?

_____

5 marks

Marks.......... /5

Using a Dictionary

Challenge 3

1 Choose the correct definition number that explains how the word 'lean' is used in these sentences.

> **lean:**
> 1. to rest against.
> 2. to bend from an upright position.
> 3. having no surplus fat.
> 4. involving difficulty or hardship.

a) He decided to lean against the fence as he needed a rest.

_____

b) Money was short so the family was having a lean time.

_____

c) Priya had to lean over to pick up the ball. _____

d) Jack Sprat could eat no fat, so he was very lean. _____

 4 marks

2 Choose the correct definition number that explains how the word 'profile' is used in these sentences.

> **profile:**
> 1. a side view or outline.
> 2. a short biographical piece of information about someone.

a) The writer was asked to give his profile to the editor so that she could put it on the cover of the book. _____

b) His profile was considered to be very elegant. _____

 2 marks

Marks.......... /6

Total marks .... /17   How am I doing?

Using a Thesaurus

1 A thesaurus is usually organised in alphabetical order and gives you words that are the same or similar in meaning to the one you have looked up. Here are some words from a thesaurus. Choose the word that you feel fits the sentence best from the choice given.

> **fright:** alarm, dismay, terrify.
> **custom:** habit, manner, routine.
> **play:** frolic, take part, act.

a) The star was to _____ in a scene from Macbeth.

b) The worried mum heard the _____ and hoped her children were safe.

c) It was their _____ to talk slowly to each other.

d) Dan heard the news about the motorway traffic jam with some

_____ as his brother was driving home on that route.

e) The children were seen to _____ in the water and were quite wet when they got home.

5 marks

Marks.......... /5

1 Circle the word that can replace the one underlined in the sentence.

a) It was a <u>bright</u> (pleasant, sunny, warm) day so we sunbathed.

Using a Thesaurus

b) Their <u>house</u> (base, haunt, dwelling) was deep in the heart of the forest.

c) He was too <u>shaky</u> (anaemic, weak, uncertain) to walk by himself.

d) Jasmine knew she had to <u>get</u> (persuade, advise, cajole) her father to let her go to Scout camp.

e) The Scouts had to <u>arm</u> (prepare, equip, attire) themselves with all the supplies they would need for their trip.

5 marks

Marks.......... /5

Challenge 3

1 Choose the best words to fit the spaces left in the passage.

battle	content	fight	truce	grief
arm	sad	harmony	weapons	

Once, many years ago, the men of my village were told to

_____ themselves ready for _____. No-one wanted to

do this as they had lived in _____ for many years with their

neighbours. They had made a _____ years before and did

not want to cause _____ for their friends. They refused to

go to war and peace was maintained.

5 marks

Marks.......... /5

Total marks .... /15   How am I doing?

Progress Test 2

Grammar

P Punctuation

S Spelling

GP **1.** Read the text and put in the correct beginning or ending of the word. Then rewrite the whole passage correctly.

Sam loved reading stories on his tablet. He had _____turned from school and immediate_____ found an exciting story on his tablet. He want_____ to immerse him _____ in the story and imagine he was the hero.

Sam had a brother and a sister that he helped to look after. His brother was five and his sister was three years old. They were call_____ him. He sighed, put down his tablet and went to see what they wanted.

_____

_____

_____

_____

_____

_____

_____

5 marks

2. Answer the following questions about the text in question 1.

a) Where had Sam returned from? _____

b) What did Sam want to imagine? _____

c) Identify three facts about Sam's family. _____

_____

_____

d) What were Sam's brother and sister doing? _____

_____

e) Why did Sam sigh? _____

3. Put a suitable prefix in front of each of these words.

a) _____sect **b)** _____side

c) _____press **d)** _____way

e) _____safe **f)** _____national

g) _____deed **h)** _____science

i) _____tell **j)** _____agree

k) _____atlantic **l)** _____hale

4. Underline the suffix in each of the following words.

a) movable **b)** existence **c)** assistant

d) majority **e)** priceless **f)** sincerely

g) horrify **h)** momentous **i)** dependable

j) observant **k)** special **l)** argument

5. Put the words in the correct place in the sentence.

a) (right, write) I must _____ my letter of apology; it is the

_____ action to take.

b) (foul, fowl) The _____ fell _____ of the butcher and became his dinner.

c) (wring, ring) When she went to _____ out the

washing, the woman took off her wedding _____.

d) (hair, hare) The fur of the _____ was soft, a bit like

my _____.

e) (scent, sent) The boy bought some _____ for his sister,

which he _____ to her for her birthday.

10 marks

S **6.** Write the correct spelling beside the word.

a) acomodate   _____

b) exagerate   _____

c) parliment   _____

d) sugest   _____

e) soilder   _____

f) vehacle   _____

g) tempatature   _____

h) eqipped   _____

8 marks

7. Write the sentences correctly, putting in any apostrophes that are needed.

a) Leylas mum was unhappy; she had lost the childrens party invitations.

_____

_____

b) Jakes and Sofias invitations were also missing.

_____

c) The football teams fans crowded into the stands to watch the match.

_____

_____

d) My teams kit was lost so they played in their tracksuits.

_____

e) Id like to hear her sing because shes got a good voice.

_____

f) Lets go and ask our friends if they will join our team.

_____

9 marks

Audience and Purpose

1 Read the extracts and underline the audiences they are written to attract.

A 'Henry Hippo lived in sunny Africa.

He was a happy hippo who enjoyed wallowing in his muddy puddle.

It was a very large puddle!'

Audience: adults, older children, young children, parents/carers

---

B Would you please ensure that your children wear correct school uniform every day? Some children are being allowed to attend school dressed in jeans and sweatshirts. This is not appropriate clothing for school.

Audience: adults, older children, young children, parents/carers

---

C 'I sailed on the Norwegian ship *Selbo* in 1942. My last sailing was in 1942 when I was eighteen. It was a Merchant navy cargo ship packed stem to stern with four-gallon cans filled with petrol. The holds were filled full with these cans. We had arrived in Algiers on 10th November 1942 and were at anchor there until 28th with German aircraft trying to sink us.'

Harold's story

Audience: adults, older children, young children, parents/carers

---

D Do you want to get fit? Come to The Fitness Gym on London Road and try our getting fit session on Wednesday evening. Free entry to those who are visiting us for the first time. Suitable for the over 50s.

Audience: adults, older children, young children, parents/carers

4 marks

Marks.......... /4

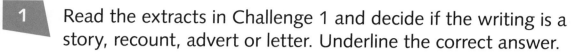

Audience and Purpose

Challenge 2

1 Read the extracts in Challenge 1 and decide if the writing is a story, recount, advert or letter. Underline the correct answer.

a) Extract A is a story, recount, advert, letter.

b) Extract B is a story, recount, advert, letter.

c) Extract C is a story, recount, advert, letter.

d) Extract D is a story, recount, advert, letter.

4 marks

Marks.......... /4

Challenge 3

1 Beside each genre of writing state whether the writer should use a formal or informal writing style.

a) report writing _____

b) advertising writing _____

c) diary writing _____

d) presenting an argument _____

e) writing a book review _____

5 marks

2 Read the extract below and underline who the audience might be and whether the writing is formal or informal.

Joe was my mate, he had been my mate since we were kids together. We did everything together, and got into loads of trouble together. When we started school, we were in the same classes until our mad antics made the teachers put us into different classes. I always thought Joe would be there for me forever but life isn't like that, I learnt.

Audience: adult, older children, wide audience

Writing: formal, informal

2 marks

Marks.......... /7

Total marks .... /15

How am I doing?

Learning from Other Writers

Challenge 1

1 Read the extracts and decide whether the writer has used his/her own experience, is writing based on research, observations carried out, or is recounting a story he/she has heard. Underline the correct answer.

A Jan 26.

The last few weeks, our own and our neighbours' gardens have been haunted by a very curious Robin. The whole of the upper plumage, which in ordinary Robins is brown, shaded with olive green, is light and silvery grey in this bird.

The writer has used his/her own experience, is writing based on research, observations carried out, or is recounting a story he/she has heard.

B We were not much more than a quarter of an hour out of our ship but we saw her sink, and then I understood for the first time what was meant by a ship foundering in the sea: I must acknowledge I had hardly eyes to look up when the seamen told me she was sinking...

The writer has used his/her own experience, is writing based on research, observations carried out, or is recounting a story he/she has heard.

2 marks

Marks........../2

Challenge 2

1 Writers can write in similar ways. Read the extracts and answer the questions using words from the extracts where possible.

A When men were all asleep the snow came flying,
In large white flakes falling on the city brown,
Stealthily and perpetually settling and loosely lying,
Hushing the latest traffic of the drowsy town;

Learning from Other Writers

B When all were asleep it began to snow; snowflakes came flying down from the sky. The flakes were large and white and covered the dirty city, making it look clean. The snow made everything quiet and hushed as it settled on the drowsy town.

a) What word do both writers use to describe the town?

_____

b) What was the effect of the flakes falling on the town in both extracts? _____

c) What effect did the snow have on the town in both extracts?

_____

3 marks

Marks.......... /3

Challenge 3

1 Read the following passages and answer the questions.

> 10 Cedar Grove
> Huntsville
> HO1 2HE
> 14 December, 2014
>
> Dear James,
>
> Thank you for your kind invitation to your party on New Year's Day. I shall be delighted to attend.
>
> Yours sincerely,
>
> Alfie

a) Is the letter formal or informal? _____

b) On which side is the address written ? _____

c) Is the ending correct for a formal letter? _____

3 marks

Marks.......... /3

Total marks .... /8

How am I doing?

71

Settings, Character and Plot

Challenge 1

1 Underline the setting(s) you think these stories should have.

    a) A story about a historical character – description of place, background of character, historical setting.

    b) A biography – description of place, background of character, historical setting.

    c) A travel guide – description of place, background of character, historical setting.

3 marks

Marks.........../3

Challenge 2

1 Read the extracts and underline what the writer is doing.

A Near the source of the Seltz, on the left bank of the Rhine, some leagues from the imperial city of Worms, there begins a range of mountains, the scattered and rugged summits of which disappear northward like a herd of wild buffaloes vanishing in a mist.

The writer is describing a scene, beginning to tell a story (narrative), showing the reader a character.

B One of the most prominent individuals hereafter connected with the Pilgrims – was Captain Myles Standish, a man whose iron nerve and dauntless energy of character went far towards carrying the infant society though the perils with which it was menaced;

The writer is describing a scene, beginning to tell a story (narrative), showing the reader a character.

Settings, Character and Plot

C If anybody cares to read a simple tale told simply, I, John Ridd, of the parish of Oare, in the county of Somerset, yeoman and churchwarden, have seen and had a share in some doings of this neighbourhood, which I will try to set down in order, God sparing my life and memory.

The writer is describing a scene, beginning to tell a story (narrative), showing the reader a character.

3 marks

Marks............/3

Challenge 3

1 Look at the plot planning points for the story. Identify the points that should go at the **beginning**, **middle** and **end** of the story.

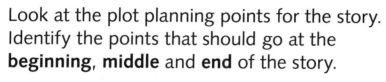

a) Return to camp _____

b) Set the scene and describe the setting of the camp

_____

c) Introduce the main characters _____

d) Tell the reader what is happening _____

e) Explore the camp _____

f) Meet the camp leaders _____

g) Arrive at the camp _____

h) See someone burying something _____

i) Search the area _____

j) Packing what they need _____

k) Escape from the thieves _____

l) Find the stolen treasure and collect reward _____

12 marks

Marks........../12

Total marks .... /18

How am I doing?

Settings, Character and Plot

G Grammar   P Punctuation   S Spelling

Challenge 1

1 Look at the sentences and underline who is telling the story.

a)
I was walking home one dark and dreary evening in winter when I realised I was not alone!   **character / writer**

b)
The evening wind was blowing and he felt cold and hungry. He was lost.   **character / writer**

2 marks

2 Answer the following questions by circling the answer.

a) What person is used when the character is relating the story?

third   first

b) When the writer is telling a story about other people, what person do they write in?

first   third

2 marks

Marks.......... /4

Challenge 2

GP **1** Read these descriptions and underline three words – adjectives or adverbs – that give information about those described.

a) James was a redheaded man who liked to ride and run through the green forests. He had green eyes and was always dressed in brown clothes.

b) I have blonde hair and blue eyes. My mother likes to dress me in pink all the time, which I don't like.

c) 'The blear-eyed, the hare-lipped, the crooked foot...'

d) He was a giant grey rat with a scarred body. He frightened all who saw him.

e) She was a swift runner, and her father often used her to deliver messages. She was small and neat, which was unusual for her family.

15 marks

Marks......... /15

Settings, Character and Plot

Challenge 3

1 Circle the correct answers.

a) What sort of atmosphere does the writer of a ghost story need to create?

| happy | sad | scary |

b) What sort of language is used in a science fiction story?

| comic | scientific | fantastic |

c) In what person is an autobiography written?

| third | first |

3 marks

2 Read the extracts and put them in the correct order to make a short story.

| **beginning** | **middle** | **end** |

a) Terrified, we dashed back to the river to help her. We couldn't find any trace of her but suddenly there was a shout and she was found safe and wet clinging to a low-lying branch. She was saved! _____

b) We had decided to walk along the forest track as it was quicker. We three sisters set off chatting and laughing.

_____

c) We didn't see the loose plank in the footbridge. As we crossed the footbridge it moved and our eldest sister toppled into the fast-moving water. We ran to get help.

_____

3 marks

Marks.......... /6

Total marks .... /25   How am I doing?

Organising Your Writing

G Grammar   P Punctuation   S Spelling

Challenge 1

1   Look at the drafting plan and put the points that a writer should always think about before writing under each heading.

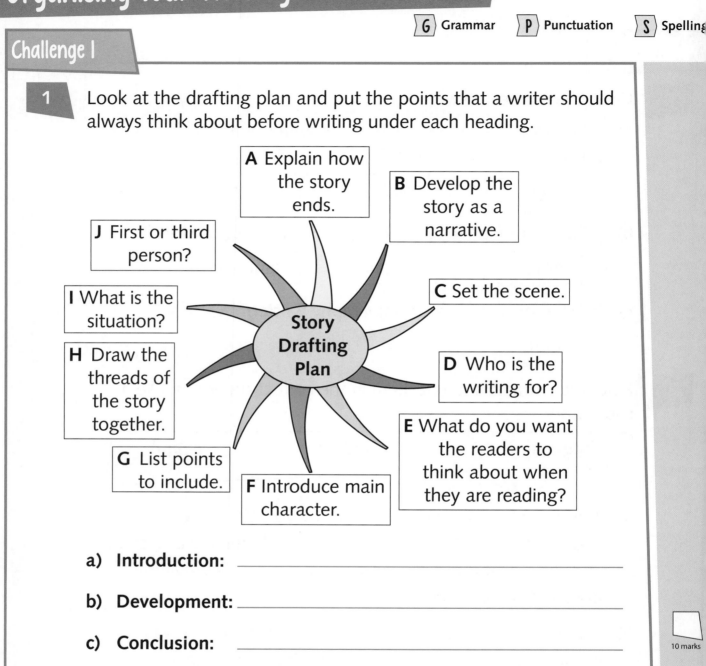

A Explain how the story ends.

B Develop the story as a narrative.

J First or third person?

I What is the situation?

C Set the scene.

Story Drafting Plan

H Draw the threads of the story together.

D Who is the writing for?

E What do you want the readers to think about when they are reading?

G List points to include.

F Introduce main character.

a) **Introduction:** _____

b) **Development:** _____

c) **Conclusion:** _____

10 marks

Marks......... /10

Challenge 2

PS   1   Read the draft and correct any errors of spelling and punctuation. You need to find one full stop, one comma, three capital letters and five spellings.

Organising Your Writing

Further down the tree lived mrs Lively the squirel. She could nearly always be seen hurrying hear and there looking for provisions to put in her hiding places for winter wake ups. she was good at collecting nuts and seeds that fell from the trees in the clearing. She stored them for their winter hiberation. Her daughter helped her and looked after the dray. The day looked messy as squirrels use lots of twigs to make their homes They are not too fussed about how the outside looks so long as they are warm and comfortable inside and can sleep peacefully and safely when they hiberate. the squirrels lived in a dray that was tucked away in a sheltered nook in the branches of the oak tree.

10 marks

Marks......... /10

Challenge 3

1 The sentences in this short story are not in the correct order. Put the letters in the correct order on the line below so that the story makes sense.

A It was the ancient pike – a large and dangerous predator!

B The girl and boy were enjoying swimming in the lake.

C "That was close," gasped the girl. "If the ancient pike had caught up with us he might have grabbed our net and taken our supper!"

D The sun shone and the wind whispered gently through the trees.

E The children did not stop to think. They swam to the shore as quickly as they could manage.

F The children were looking at the fish swimming below them when suddenly they saw a large shadow emerge from behind a rock.

Order of sentences: _____

6 marks

Marks.......... /6

Total marks .... /26   How am I doing?

Organising your Writing

Challenge 1

G **1** Read the passage and underline the conjunction or adverbial in each pair that makes sense.

> The Headteacher was speaking in assembly **because/therefore** he was concerned about the pupils' safety on the busy road outside the school. **In particular/Indeed**, he thought it was important for the children to wear reflective clothing. He had some pupils modelling the reflective clothing that he wanted to make part of their uniform, **especially/as** he wanted them to see how well it worked in poor light. **In the same way/Like** he had children model the non reflective coats **so that/consequently** they would see how difficult it was to see them in poor light.

5 marks

Marks.......... /5

Challenge 2

G **1** Here is a passage that should be in two paragraphs. Read the passage and underline the first sentence of the second paragraph.

> I married my husband Joe in 1936 when I was twenty-one. He was twenty-two. We had been offered a bungalow that would cost £350 to buy. We couldn't afford it and moved into rented rooms that cost us 9 shillings a week. We had £4 a week to live on so we had to be very careful with our budget. I remember when War was declared and Joe was called up. All those men going to fight far away from home. I was sad to wave Joe off at the station, especially as I didn't know when I would see him again.

a) List four conjunctions. _____ , _____ ,

_____ , _____

b) When does the story begin? _____

6 marks

Marks.......... /

Organising your Writing

1 Read this detailed description of a man. Put a tick after the sentences below that you feel describe the man.

Upon hearing this he appeared satisfied and consented to come on board. Good God! Margaret, if you had seen the man who thus capitulated for his safety, your surprise would have been boundless. His limbs were nearly frozen, and his body dreadfully emaciated by fatigue and suffering. I never saw a man in so wretched a condition. We attempted to carry him into the cabin, but as soon as he had quitted the fresh air he fainted. We accordingly brought him back to the deck and restored him to animation by rubbing him with brandy and forcing him to swallow a small quantity. As soon as he showed signs of life we wrapped him up in blankets and placed him near the chimney of the kitchen stove. By slow degrees he recovered and ate a little soup, which restored him wonderfully.

Letter from Captain Robert Walton who is sailing his ship to the North Pole.

a) The man was extremely cold.

b) The man was heavy and strong looking.

c) The man was thin and starving.

d) He was in a bad state.

e) He was lively and chatted to us.

f) He had a large drink of brandy.

g) He fainted when he was taken below deck.

4 marks

Marks.......... /4

Total marks .... /15

How am I doing?

Précis

Challenge 1

1 Read the text and pick out the three main points.

> The Mole had been working very hard all the morning, spring-cleaning his little home. First with brooms, then with dusters; then on ladders and steps and chairs, with a brush and a pail of whitewash; till he had dust in his throat and eyes, and splashes of whitewash all over his black fur, and an aching back and weary arms. Spring was moving in the air above and in the earth below and around him, penetrating even his dark and lowly little house with its spirit of divine discontent and longing.

a) _____

b) _____

c) _____

d) What is the writing describing in detail? _____

_____

e) What was Spring doing? _____

_____

5 marks

Marks.......... /5

Challenge 2

1 Read the article and underline the main point in each sentence.

> Joseph was twenty-five years old when he became a soldier. He looked very handsome in his uniform and his widowed mother was proud of him. In 1914 he went to war. He knew the horrors of the trenches and learned that war was horrific. His letters home were always cheerful as he did not want to worry his mother.

Précis

He fought in the Battle of the Somme and survived but lost a leg in the battle. He was sent home to recover and to the delight of his mother played no further part in the war. The war ended in 1918 and Joseph had lost many dear friends. He thought war a terrible thing and did not want his sons or grandsons to ever have to go through such suffering.

8 marks

Marks.......... /8

Challenge 3

1 Here is a précis of the passage about Joseph in Challenge 2. Put the sentences in the correct order.

A He thought war terrible and did not want his sons or grandsons to go through such suffering.

B He was sent home as he had lost a leg.

C Joseph was twenty five when he became a soldier.

D The war ended in 1918.

E Joseph had lost many dear friends.

F He fought in and survived the Battle of the Somme.

G He knew the horror of the trenches.

H In 1914 he went to war.

I He did not tell his mother about the trenches when he wrote home.

Order of sentences:

_____

9 marks

Marks......... /9

Total marks .... /22   How am I doing?

Proofreading

Grammar   Punctuation   Spelling

Challenge 1

S **1** Read the passage and underline the 10 spelling mistakes. Spell the words correctly in the space provided at the end of the passage.

Helo, you might be wondering who I am or what I am. Let me tell you. I am a dinorsaur! I live in a world that is very diferent to yours. You might recognise some of the plants that I see every day but many would be strange to you. I live in a world of coniferos forests, groves of cycads and fern-like plants. Flowering plants like magnolia, holly, ginkgo, dogwood, horsetails and ferns make my world beautiful.

Dinosaurs like me can be found in the areas you now call North America and Euurope. There are large freswater lakes where England and the South of France will be. I live in the Cretaceous period and dinosaurs are large pant eaters or meat eaters. I am a herbivore which means that I am a plant-eating dinosaur. My herd name is Triceraatops. I have a short, strong neck that makes it eesy for me to pull at and eat tough vegetation. I have three horns that I can figt with and I live in a herd that roams the countryside. We get to know the land and find out where there are good places to visit and where the eating is good.

a) _____ b) _____

c) _____ d) _____

e) _____ f) _____

g) _____ h) _____

i) _____ j) _____

10 marks

Marks......... /10

Challenge 2

G **1** Underline the incorrect verb form and write the correct verb form in the space at the end of the sentence.

a) The teacher checked that the homework were handed in.

_____

Proofreading

b) I done my homework last night. _____

c) They remembered that they has left their umbrellas on the bus.

_____

d) If I would have worked harder I would have passed my test.

_____

e) The book were very good,
I really enjoyed the story.

_____

5 marks

Marks.......... /5

Challenge 3

1 Read the following passage and underline the mistakes.
Write the passage out correctly. There are 15 mistakes to find.

Helen was a keen football player. she were a good
member of the girl's team. I remeber the first time i saw
her play. She was the centre-forward and score a brilliant
gol she will probable play for england won day! I will
look fourward to that day and make sure I go to wach the match

_____

_____

_____

_____

_____

_____

_____

_____

15 marks

Marks......... /15

Total marks .... /30   How am I doing?

83

Progress Test 3

S **1.** Fill in the blanks with the correct silent letters. There is a blank for each missing letter.

    a) fir_e_   **b)** si_g_n

    c) clim_b_   **d)** rig_h_t

    e) fr_i_end

5 marks

2. Read each sentence and identify the audience it is aimed at.

young children	older children	mixed audience

    a) The hungry hippo ate lots of jelly, but that did not fill him up! _____

    b) Please turn off your mobile phones before the film begins. _____

    c) The fantastic four thought that to make a den you needed wood, leaves, string and a plan! _____

    d) The big bear was unhappy that someone had sat in his chair. _____

    e) To get fit you must eat healthily and do more exercise. Join our keep fit club! _____

5 marks

3. Decide if the writing is formal, informal, recounting, descriptive or persuasive.

    a) Dear Diary – today was really bad! I got my ticket for the match and it wasn't the seat I wanted! _____

    b) To construct the box, follow the instructions as they are written. _____

    c) You really need to think about buying the scarf, as it really suits your colouring. _____

    d) Yesterday, we walked to school with our friends. The sun shone on the lake making the waves glisten and sparkle; we thought it would be fun to go for a swim. _____

4 marks

4. Write a letter in each space to complete the word.

   a) Animals running in fear is called a st_mp_d_.

   b) A group of people make up a co_ _ un _ ty.

   c) Thunder and li_ _ t_ing go together.

   d) It was the tw_l_th day of Christmas.

   e) N_ _ ghb_ _rs are the people who live nearby.

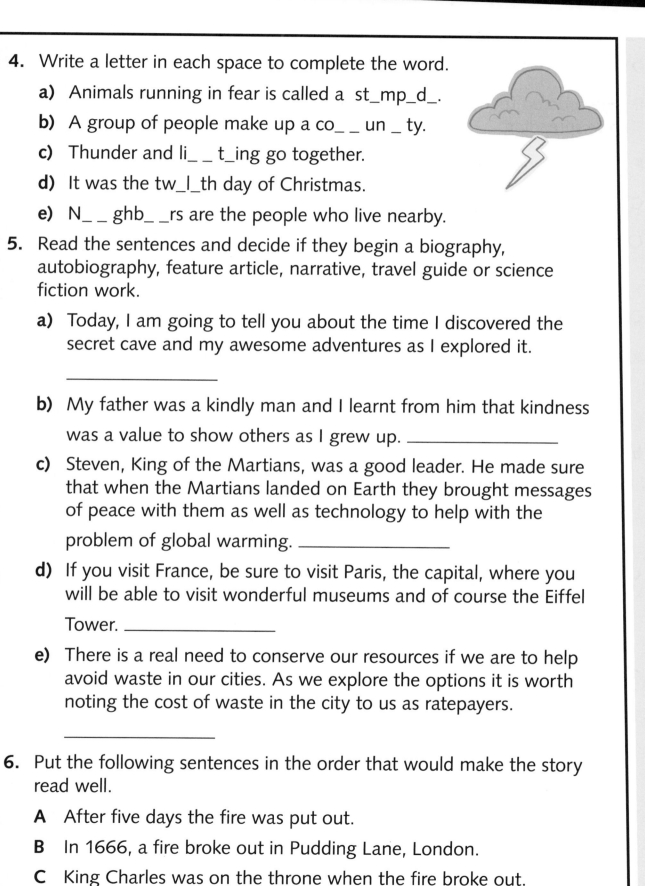

5 marks

5. Read the sentences and decide if they begin a biography, autobiography, feature article, narrative, travel guide or science fiction work.

   a) Today, I am going to tell you about the time I discovered the secret cave and my awesome adventures as I explored it.

   _____

   b) My father was a kindly man and I learnt from him that kindness was a value to show others as I grew up. _____

   c) Steven, King of the Martians, was a good leader. He made sure that when the Martians landed on Earth they brought messages of peace with them as well as technology to help with the problem of global warming. _____

   d) If you visit France, be sure to visit Paris, the capital, where you will be able to visit wonderful museums and of course the Eiffel Tower. _____

   e) There is a real need to conserve our resources if we are to help avoid waste in our cities. As we explore the options it is worth noting the cost of waste in the city to us as ratepayers.

   _____

5 marks

6. Put the following sentences in the order that would make the story read well.

   A After five days the fire was put out.

   B In 1666, a fire broke out in Pudding Lane, London.

   C King Charles was on the throne when the fire broke out.

D The city was rebuilt by Sir Christopher Wren.

E He ordered that firebreaks should be made to try and stop the fire spreading.

F Many homes were destroyed by the fire.

G As well as homes Old Saint Paul's Cathedral burned down.

Order of sentences:

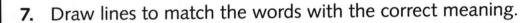

7 marks

7. Draw lines to match the words with the correct meaning.

a)
exaggerate

to make greater

to make up a story

b)
programme

written or published list of events

a computer instruction

c)
system

a method or set method

an electrical chart

d)
ancient

dating from very long ago

a people living in modern times

4 marks

8. Read the following passage and list the five important facts you would include in a précis.

Windsor Castle is a famous castle and has been the residence of Royal families for over 900 years. It began as a wooden Motte built by William the Conqueror and is now a massive stone fortress. Windsor Castle was nearly destroyed by fire in 1992 and over 100 rooms were devastated by the fire. Great efforts were made to save the valuable paintings that were in the castle. Firefighters and members of the Royal family worked hard to let people know what was happening and eventually the building was restored at no cost to the taxpayer. There are other famous castles but Windsor Castle is the one near London that the Royal family go to. It is where members of their family are buried.

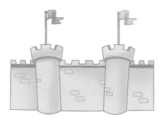

a) _____

b) _____

c) _____

d) _____

e) _____

5 marks

9. Underline the word whose meaning best fits the sentence.

a) He **requested/begged** that he be let home early for his appointment.

b) The firefighters **wished/hoped** to save the person in the burning house.

c) The queen thought the man was very **brave/strong** to rescue the boy from the sea.

d) The children **left/abandoned** the treehouse when they became interested in computer games.

4 marks

Marks.........../44

Verbs

Challenge 1

G **1** Read the sentence, underline the verb and underline what it does in the sentence.

a) The cheetah ran after the gazelle.
Describes an action, mental state, state of being.

b) Daniel was unhappy in the lion's den.
Describes an action, mental state, state of being.

c) Marie felt lonely by herself in the park.
Describes an action, mental state, state of being.

d) The girls were reading their books.
Describes an action, mental state, state of being.

e) The dragon roared loudly.
Describes an action, mental state,
state of being.

10 marks

Marks......... /10

Challenge 2

G **1** Verbs can be written in different tenses. State whether the sentences are in the **past**, **present** or **future tense**.

a) The fairies danced in the moonlight last night. _____

b) He is playing with his train set. _____

c) Tomorrow, we will ride our horses to the beach. _____

3 marks

G **2** Put the correct version of the verb 'to be' in the sentences.

a) We _____ walking to school very slowly.

b) Everyone _____ tired after their marathon run
yesterday.

c) _____ we going back home now our holiday is over?

d) Yesterday they _____ playing 'Pin the tail on the donkey' at the party.

e) Today she _____ playing football for the school team.

5 marks

Marks.......... /8

Challenge 3

1 Rewrite the sentences correctly in the tense indicated.

a) I am writing my story.

Future _____

b) I cooked my tea and thought I might eat it outside.

Present _____

c) Hardeep will be playing goalkeeper for the hockey team.

Past _____

d) He brewed his mum a cup of tea.

Future _____

e) The plane was late taking off for London.

Present _____

5 marks

Marks.......... /5

Total marks .... /23

How am I doing?

Verbs

Challenge 1

G **1** Put the correct verbs in each sentence to make it make sense.

woke	would	call	ringing	to sign
thought	played	were	had been	

a) The alarm _____ loudly _____ me up for school.

b) _____ the boss, she needs _____ the letter urgently!

c) If he _____ in charge the game would be _____ in the rain.

d) The Smith family _____ _____ travelling on the train for hours.

e) Jake _____ he _____ enjoy the stew and apple pie for dinner.

5 marks

Marks.......... /5

Challenge 2

G **1** Read the sentence and circle the correct verb.

a) The doors **is/are** open today.

b) I counted my money and **realised/realise** that I need to save more.

c) The Lord Mayor **was/were** planning a visit to our school.

d) Ollie and Alex **have/has** a book about origami.

e) Their birthday cards **arrives/arrived** on the actual day of their birthday.

5 marks

Marks.......... /5

1 Read the poem and underline the four verbs that tell us what the eagle is doing.

> He clasps the crag with crooked hands;
> Close to the sun in lonely lands,
> Ring'd with the azure world, he stands.
>
> The wrinkled sea beneath him crawls;
> He watches from his mountain walls,
> And like a thunderbolt he falls.

4 marks

2 Use the correct forms of the verbs in the boxes below in the spaces left in the passage.

| stun | have | make | is | see |

> Jones, the baker, liked making cakes. He _____ little
>
> and large cakes. The best cake _____ a purple one for
>
> a wedding. It _____ three tiers and _____ all who
>
> _____ it with its magnificence.

5 marks

Marks.......... /9

Total marks .... /19

How am I doing?

Adverbs

Challenge 1

 1 Underline the adverb in the sentence which tells **when**, **where**, **how** or **why**. The first one has been done for you.

a) The farmer <u>carefully</u> walked through the field with the bull in it. <u>How</u>

b) Mathias slowly tiptoed past Cluny, the rat. _____

c) As darkness fell, the guard began shouting hourly. _____

d) The castle ramparts frequently collapsed as they were old.

_____

e) They roughly threw the prisoners into the deepest cells.

_____

f) The teacher always called the register at the beginning of the day. _____

10 marks

Marks.........../10

Challenge 2

 1 Read the passage and underline the adverbs.

> Yesterday I worked hard to make the salad for lunch.
> I carefully washed the lettuce, cucumber and spring onions.
> I hard boiled four eggs and after I had cooled them, I slowly peeled them. I quickly chopped the lettuce, cucumber and spring onions and placed them on the plates. The eggs were cut in half and I carelessly placed them on top of the greens. The salad was ready for my guests.

6 marks

Marks.........../6

Adverbs

Challenge 3

1 Write the missing adverbs in the spaces in a) to e). Then choose an adverb listed in a) to e) to use in the sentences in f) to j).

a) hard, _____, hardest

b) _____, better, best

c) small, smaller, _____

d) far, _____, furthest

e) much, more, _____

f) The team tried _____ after half time.

g) He was the _____ hopeful he had ever been when he opened his exam results.

h) She was the _____ of them, yet the most loved.

i) The children were the _____ from home any of them had ever been.

j) The team practised their game and soon they were the _____ team in the league.

10 marks

Marks........ /10

Total marks .... /26

How am I doing?

Modal Verbs

G Grammar   **P** Punctuation   **S** Spelling

G **1** Underline the modal verbs in the sentences.

a) In Finland it snows in winter so it must be very cold outside.

b) They couldn't carry the logs because they were too heavy.

c) My granddaughter can speak two languages: English and Finnish.

d) The shoppers hurry to the sales for they must have the latest bargains.

e) He asked if he could leave later as he had to finish his dinner.

5 marks

Marks.......... /5

G **1** Write the correct modal verb in the space.

can	could	can't	couldn't
must	mustn't	needn't	

a) Dad has agreed, so we _____ go to the park today to practise our skate-boarding.

b) We _____ go fishing today as it's too cold.

c) The man told his son that he _____ clean the car as it was going to rain.

d) They _____ find the key to the car in the usual places.

e) Amba kindly said that they _____ borrow her space fiction story as it was such a good read.

5 marks

Marks.......... /5

Modal Verbs

Challenge 3

1 Tick the statement that follows the sentence best.

a) The car you bought is very up to date.

It must be a very good drive. ☐

It can't have been a good drive. ☐

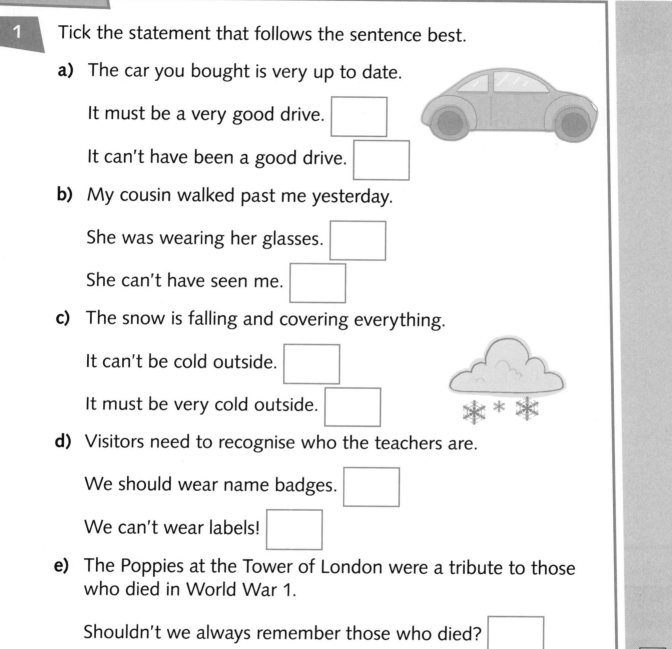

b) My cousin walked past me yesterday.

She was wearing her glasses. ☐

She can't have seen me. ☐

c) The snow is falling and covering everything.

It can't be cold outside. ☐

It must be very cold outside. ☐

d) Visitors need to recognise who the teachers are.

We should wear name badges. ☐

We can't wear labels! ☐

e) The Poppies at the Tower of London were a tribute to those who died in World War 1.

Shouldn't we always remember those who died? ☐

I can't remember why they put them there. ☐

5 marks

Marks.......... /5

Total marks .... /15

How am I doing?

Noun Phrases

 G Grammar   **P** Punctuation   **S** Spelling

Challenge 1

G **1** Complete each sentence using the end of the sentence from the box below that fits the noun phrase best.

> is built for racing.
> helped us to understand the culture of the country better.
> was very happy when his family asked him to stay with them.
> can fill the heart with joy.
> ran the relay race skilfully and swiftly.

a) The four friends _____

b) The old man _____

_____

c) My boat _____

d) A beautiful sunset _____

e) The language lesson _____

_____

 5 marks

Marks.......... /5

Challenge 2

G **1** Underline the noun phrases in the following sentences.

a) The big boy was wearing his new trainers on the running track.

b) Sylvester the cat chased his enemy around the house.

Noun Phrases

c) All the animals were hiding.

d) The best defence against sunburn is strong lotion.

e) Amelia likes galloping on her horse.

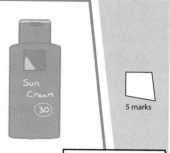

5 marks

Marks.......... /5

Challenge 3

1 Change the meaning of the underlined noun phrase into the opposite of the original. Rewrite the whole sentence.

a) <u>The happy girl</u> went to school with her friend.

_____

b) <u>The tidy boy</u> put his clothes away.

_____

c) <u>The beautiful princess</u> married the attractive prince.

_____

d) <u>The sad children</u> ran to their mother for a hug.

_____

e) <u>My new tablet</u> works better than this one does.

_____

_____

5 marks

Marks.......... /5

otal marks .... /15

How am I doing?

Sentences

G Grammar   P Punctuation   S Spelling

Challenge 1

GP **1** Join the two simple sentences with an appropriate word.

| however | meanwhile | alternatively |
| because | consequently |

a) The dog is panting. It is thirsty.

_____

b) The children worked hard. Their teacher prepared a treat for them.

_____

_____

c) Noah wanted a dog. His mum didn't want one.

_____

d) I bought a big bag of logs from the market. I could not carry it home. It was so heavy.

_____

_____

e) You need to have a bath. You can have a shower or a sauna.

_____

5 marks

Marks.......... /

Challenge 2

1 Identify which sentences are active or passive.

a) The boy sang loudly in the choir. _____

b) The choir was conducted by the choirmaster. _____

Sentences

c) Lewis Carroll wrote the book *Alice in Wonderland*. _____

d) The *Matilda* was shipwrecked a long time ago. _____

e) Red lights were put up by the traffic police.

_____

5 marks

Marks.......... /5

Challenge 3

1 Change each sentence into the active voice.

a) The birthday cake was decorated by granddad.

_____

b) Coloured balls were used by the team for their hockey practice.

_____

c) The windows had been washed by his dad.

_____

d) The tea was drunk by Mrs Plumb, the vicar's wife.

_____

e) Crisp packets and sweet wrappers were blown around the square by the wind.

_____

5 marks

Marks.......... /5

Total marks .... /15   How am I doing?

Relative Clauses

Challenge 1

 1 Use a relative pronoun to join the two sentences together.

| which | where | that | whose | who |

a) I like the dog. The dog lives next door.

_____

b) The young boy is happy. His football was found.

_____

c) I live in Manchester. I go to school in Manchester.

_____

d) The house I live in has a garden. It is very large.

_____

e) Mr Smith has a daughter. She is a doctor.

_____

5 marks

Marks.......... /5

Challenge 2

 1 Complete the sentences with a relative pronoun.

 who   whom   whose   where

a) What is the address of the boy _____ sports kit you borrowed?

Relative Clauses

b) A cinema is a building _____ people go to see films.

c) I do know the name of the officer to _____ I spoke yesterday.

d) A grocer is a person _____ sells vegetables in his shop.

4 marks

Marks.......... /4

Challenge 3

1 Put the correct relative pronouns in the sentences.

a) Ruth and Fergus, _____ (who, that) got married last summer, are going on holiday to France.

b) The place _____ (who, that) they are going to is a holiday flat.

c) The holiday, _____ (which, what) they booked in autumn, was a bargain.

d) The clerk _____ (whom, whose) company they booked through won a prize for selling the most holidays that week.

e) His boss to _____ (whom, who) he spoke yesterday plans to promote him.

5 marks

Marks.......... /5

Total marks .... /14

How am I doing?

Commas

G) Grammar   P) Punctuation   S) Spelling

Challenge I

GP) 1 Rewrite the sentences, adding commas to make the meaning clear.

a) I went to the shops and bought apples oranges bread and butter but I forgot the milk tea and sugar.

_____

b) The band leader walked to the front took out his baton and started to conduct the band.

_____

c) His dad was a happy cheerful man.

_____

d) We wanted to go to the beach so we packed a picnic and left.

_____

4 marks

Marks.......... /4

Challenge 2

GP) 1 Rewrite the sentences, adding commas around the additional information.

a) Mr Smith the butcher parcelled up the meat we had ordered.

_____

b) The thief who was sneaking around outside decided not to break in after all.

_____

c) The children who were all present were excited about the visit to the zoo.

_____

3 marks

Marks.......... /3

Commas

Challenge 3

1 Rewrite the following and put commas and inverted commas in the correct places.

a) 1256 _____

b) January 20th 2015 _____

c) Tomorrow we will go back to school Shanti said.

_____

_____

d) In spring the plants begin to grow again.

_____

_____

4 marks

2 Some of the sentences are punctuated incorrectly or have punctuation missing. Put a cross at the end of the incorrect sentences and a tick at the end of the correct ones.

a) The father suggested that they go to the park, and that they played football. ☐

b) The band, conducted by Tilly, played well. ☐

c) I am going to sing, but not on the stage. ☐

d) We are eating fish chips and peas. ☐

e) We go back to school on 20th October. ☐

5 marks

Marks.........../9

Total marks ..../16   How am I doing?

103

Hyphens, Dashes and Brackets

Challenge 1

P **1** Rewrite the sentences inserting hyphens correctly.

a) The teacher made them re enter the room less noisily.

_____

b) The parents knew when their children misbehaved because they were all seeing.

_____

c) Their son in law was a very tall man.

_____

d) The sailor told the story of the man eating shark being seen in the bay.

_____

e) He designed an amazing Tshirt for the band to wear.

_____

5 marks

Marks.......... /5

Challenge 2

P **1** Rewrite the sentences putting in dashes where needed.

a) The film was amazing an excellent experience!

_____

b) How how did you manage that?

_____

c) We found the children they were very happy indeed.

_____

Hyphens, Dashes and Brackets

d) The pony the second his owners had bought got lost one day.

_____

e) My daughter-in-law has reworked her design for our living room it's amazing!

_____

5 marks

Marks.......... /5

Challenge 3

1 Put brackets in the sentences to make them more effective.

a) Mum's computer was green bright green with a bright green cover.

b) They were going on holiday for the first time to Greece.

c) Bert and Daisy were early unlike yesterday, so the meal began on time.

d) The boy's story *My Adventures in Space* was displayed in the school library.

e) The poet Coleridge he wrote *The Ancient Mariner* lived in the Lake District.

5 marks

Marks.......... /5

Total marks .... /15

How am I doing?

Semicolons, Colons and Bullet Points

G Grammar   **P** Punctuation   **S** Spelling

Challenge 1

P **1** Insert the semicolons in the sentences.

a) We are selling our house we want someone to buy it soon.

b) The lion survived the operation on its leg however, it limped for a long time afterwards.

c) Andy owned a cat, a dog, and a pony he kept them in a specially-built wooden house.

d) *The Long, Short and the Tall The Incredibles The Magic Faraway Tree* are all films I have seen.

e) Marie, the taller of the two, was able to reach the shelf we were all pleased as we could now have a biscuit.

5 marks

Marks.......... /5

Challenge 2

P **1** Insert colons where they are needed.

a) I wrote my shopping list ten eggs, a kilo of sugar, a kilo of flour and some dried fruit.

b) Please give the following information your name, occupation, age.

c) The flight leaves at 13 40 hours.

d) The ballot results were announced Ruth was the new team leader.

e) To get there I had to run all day the distance was daunting.

f) You are going to read verses from *Macbeth* Scene 2 lines 1 6.

g) I want to know everything the date, time and place.

7 marks

Marks.......... /7

Semicolons, Colons and Bullet Points

Challenge 3

1 Rewrite the following using bullet points, taking in a colon before them.

a) For their sports day the children had the following egg-and-spoon races hop, skip and jump parents' races.

_____

_____

_____

_____

b) The holiday bungalow was lovely but lacked a few basic items towels blankets washing powder.

_____

_____

_____

_____

c) The town was interesting for tourists but some things were best to leave out swimming in the lake eating uncooked food buying tourist souvenirs.

_____

_____

_____

_____

9 marks

Marks......... /9

Total marks .... /21   How am I doing?

G 1. Read the passage and underline the verbs in it.

> The woman was standing on the deck of the boat. She felt the boat turn and suddenly she was in the sea swimming to shore. She took a deep breath. Then a strong hand grabbed her. She was pulled into a small rowing boat, she was saved!

12 marks

G 2. What tenses are these sentences written in?

a) The dog runs swiftly to its owner. _____

b) My family and friends went to the

seaside yesterday. _____

c) Daisy and Mark were good friends

who enjoyed playing football

together. _____

d) We will be playing tennis during the summer months.

_____

e) I am making a cake for tea. _____

5 marks

G 3. Put the correct verbs in the sentences.

a) Robert _____ in charge of the computers; he _____ to mend them if they broke down.

b) Mum thought the bird with a yellow beak _____ a blackbird.

c) James _____ working hard to get the house clean.

d) I _____ planning to _____ fishing tomorrow.

e) Where _____ the box of chocolates?

5 marks

G 4. Insert the adverb that fits the sentence best.

| hardest | prolifically | slowly | backwards | beautifully |

a) My friends were singing _____ in the choir.

b) The monster walked _____ into the forest.

c) He was looking for his favourite mushrooms, which grew

_____ in the forest.

d) She jumped _____ off the diving board.

e) The students worked hard but it was the student who worked

_____ that won the prize.

5 marks

5. Choose a suitable modal verb to insert in the space.

can	could	can't	couldn't
must	need	have to	

a) We _____ have a curry for dinner today.

b) Tomorrow we _____ have a walk in the park.

c) Al _____ reach the top shelf even
though he was the tallest person in the shop.

d) _____ we go swimming tomorrow?

e) You _____ not switch the television on as you need to do
your homework.

5 marks

6. Here is the first draft of a story. Read it and underline the mistakes
and insert the three missing words. There are seven mistakes.

years ago, a family of mice lived in a hole in an oak tree. The oak

tree was on the ede of a wood, near a field. An old hedge grew near

the oak tree _____ formed the boundary of the field. The hedge

provided shelter and food for the mice and they enjoyed living in

their special place

The family _____ made up of a father mother and four babies. the baby mice kept their parents busy, as they were curious _____ always looking for adventures and fun. The ole in the oak tree was a good place to live because it was so very comforable and warm, especially in winter when the mice slept a lot.

10 marks

G **7.** Underline the noun phrases in the sentences.

a) The ancient, dilapidated house was creaking in the wind.

b) The sad child was happy when her mother returned.

c) Some monkeys were built for swinging through the trees.

d) Van Gogh's paintings can inspire the world!

4 marks

P **8.** Rewrite the passage with the correct punctuation.

jim was a smart lively boy he lived in a cottage with his mother mary jim liked helping his mother gather herbs mushrooms and leaves for the cooking pot mary and jim enjoyed making tasty meals together

_____

_____

_____

_____

_____

_____

_____

13 marks

9. Rewrite the following passage with correct punctuation.

> The football fans were excited they were going to town! Alex the leader was organising the walk to the bus stop. The group had bought special Tshirts for the trip. Alex was amazed such enthusiasm!
>
> They were on the bus they would arrive in town soon. They had to be at the stadium by 14 20 if they were to see the start of the match. The fans were all keen footballers so they said they would enjoy seeing the match.

_____

_____

_____

_____

_____

_____

_____

_____

8 marks

10. Organise the following into a list using bullet points. Remember to put a colon before the bullets.

> Please display good manners in the pool no spitting no bombing no diving

_____

_____

_____

_____

3 marks

Marks........ /70

Answers

Pages 4–11
Starter Test

1. a) The midday bus from Southsea will arrive in London in the evening.
   b) My name is Daisy and my birthday is in May.
   c) Friday is the day of the week named after the Norse goddess Freya.
   d) I was given an Apple computer for my birthday.
   e) Dr Adam Smith met and married Aida in New York. **(5 marks)**
2. Andrew; morning; Thursday; coin; Finland; cooking; Act 4; Mars **(5 marks)**
3. a) boxes   b) cows
   c) calves   d) mice
   e) women   f) hippopotami
   g) maids-of-honour h) sheep
   i) pennies   j) heroes
   (10 marks)
4. a) either...or   b) when
   c) because   d) if
   e) although   **(5 marks)**
5. Grace was a kind girl. She often shared her lunch-time snack with her friends as they liked the cakes her mother baked for her. Grace's mother was a chef and worked in the nearby hotel making wonderful meals for the guests. **(12 marks)**
6. a) "Hi there," said Colin. "Are you going to the park?"
   b) Mandy cried out, "Look out! There's a car coming!"
   c) "Are you all right?" asked the police officer, "I have the number of the car – that was very dangerous driving!"
   d) Mandy and Colin managed to reply, "We're OK thanks." **(4 marks)**
7. a) They; themselves   b) she
   c) Who   d) yours
   e) us   **(5 marks)**
8. a) disobey   b) misbehave
   c) impatiently d) rewrite
   e) autobiography **(5 marks)**
9. a) information   b) sadly
   c) measurements   d) likeable
   e) neighbourhood **(5 marks)**
10. a) address   b) believe
    c) certain   d) disappear
    e) experience f) naughty
    g) occasion   h) weight
    (8 marks)
11. a) accepted   b) broke
    c) fare   d) knot
    e) meat   f) missed
    (6 marks)
12. a) The men, women and children were leaving the village.
    b) The rains had caught them.
    c) The roofs were unmended.
    d) The rain is described as the blinding hot rain of the morning.
    e) The families heard a crash of falling beams and thatch behind the walls. **(5 marks)**
13. a) The poster is advertising a pantomime called Aladdin.
    b) Sunday
    c) Tuesday and Thursday
    d) The panto is amazing, the seats are comfortable, Abanazer is wicked.
    e) To get comfortable seats and inexpensive tickets.
    (5 marks)

Pages 12–13
Challenge 1
1. a) intercity (a fast rail service between towns)
   b) inaudible (not loud enough to be heard)
   c) disappear (to cease to be visible, to vanish)
   d) retake (to do again) **(8 marks)**
Challenge 2
1. a) unknown   b) misbehave
   c) impatiently   d) illegible
   (4 marks)

2. a) relearn   b) refurnish
   c) unlock   d) semi-retired
   (4 marks)

Challenge 3
1. unpleasant; invisible; mislead; retraced; nowhere **(5 marks)**

Pages 14–15
Challenge 1

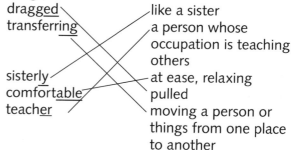

(10 marks)

Answers

Challenge 2

1. a) comfortably   b) considerably
   c) referred   d) explanation
   e) horrible   **(5 marks)**
2. a) visibly   b) preparation
   c) substantial   d) collision
                               (4 marks)

Challenge 3

1. Once, a man was <u>sitting</u> <u>patiently</u> on a chair in his kitchen. He was <u>wondering</u> what he could have for his dinner. There was nothing in the cupboard. Suddenly there was a knock at the door and in came his daughter. She placed her basket on the table and began to quickly empty it. Her father was <u>curious</u>. What was in the basket? Food began to appear on the table. The man was filled with <u>happiness</u> and thought that his daughter was <u>wonderful</u>.   **(5 marks)**

Pages 16–17
Challenge 1

1. a) chil<u>d</u><u>ren</u>; miss<u>ed</u>
   b) danger<u>ous</u>; <u>wear</u>ing
   c) <u>im</u>possible
   d) perform<u>ance</u>
   e) <u>pass</u>ing; <u>il</u>legal
   f) <u>dis</u>honest; <u>dis</u>liked   **(10 marks)**

Challenge 2

1. a) observant
   b) infectious
   c) understandable
   d) satisfying
   e) comfortable   **(5 marks)**

Challenge 3

1.

Word	Prefix	Prefix meaning
a) interchange	inter	many
b) autobiography	auto	hear
c) multipurpose	multi	outstanding
d) audition	audi	across
e) transport	trans	between, among
f) superman	super	self, own

                          (6 marks)

Pages 18–19
Challenge 1

1. a) example
   b) mythology (*or* mythical)
   c) cowboy (*or* cowgirl; cowslip; cowpat; cowlick; cower; coward)

d) minibus (*or* omnibus)
e) famous
f) television   **(5 marks)**

Challenge 2

1. a) waterworks   b) peanut
   c) notebook   d) newspaper
   e) forever   **(5 marks)**

Challenge 3

1. a) newscaster   b) stagehand
   c) fishbowl   d) warm-blooded
   e) candlelight   **(5 marks)**
2. <u>walk</u>ing; <u>tad</u>poles; <u>hop</u>ing; ruck<u>sack</u>; over<u>taken</u>; exam<u>ined</u>; <u>impress</u>ed   **(7 marks)**

Pages 20–21
Challenge 1

1. a) caring   b) huge
   c) depart   d) stroll
   e) agreeable   **(5 marks)**

Challenge 2

1. a) spied   b) evening
   c) control   d) mischief
   e) delighted   **(5 marks)**

Challenge 3

1. a) declared   b) glanced
   c) usually   d) distinguished
   e) great   **(5 marks)**

Pages 22–23
Challenge 1

1.

Word	Antonym
a) accept	decline
b) better	worse
c) cheap	expensive
d) divide	multiply
e) entrance	exit **(5 marks)**

Challenge 2

1. a) It was a <u>sunny</u> day.   rainy/dull
   b) The place on the bus for buggies was <u>occupied</u>.   empty/unoccupied/vacant
   c) "We are at <u>war</u>!" replied the General.   peace
   d) The hall was <u>empty</u>; they had thought that no-one would come to the concert.   <u>full</u>
   e) The <u>friends</u> sat down to talk things through.   enemies   **(5 marks)**

Challenge 3

1. a) The <u>little</u> girl was unable to reach the <u>big</u> pot on the shelf.
   b) When it is <u>hot</u> you should drink <u>cold</u> drinks. (*Or* When it is <u>cold</u> you should drink <u>hot</u> drinks.)

c) He liked <u>antique</u> shops even though he was <u>young</u> and poor.

d) Ben's house was <u>filthy</u> when he moved into it but he soon had it <u>shipshape</u> and tidy. **(8 marks)**

2. a) When you take a test make sure you read the <u>question</u> carefully before you select your <u>answer</u>.

b) Cinderella wore a <u>beautiful</u> dress to the ball, unlike the <u>ugly</u> dresses her stepsisters wore.

c) "Did you <u>remember</u> to go to the library or did you <u>forget</u> again?" asked her father.

d) <u>Polite</u> people are liked but <u>rude</u> people are avoided.

e) Her dad drove an <u>expensive</u> car but she only could afford a <u>cheap</u> one. **(5 marks)**

Pages 24–25
Challenge 1
1. a) real hunger meant
   b) black as a sloe
   c) deep boring grubs **(3 marks)**
Challenge 2
1. a) a sea-chest   b) plodding
   c) (soiled) blue   d) sabre **(4 marks)**
Challenge 3
1. a) Jim   b) Mowgli
   c) a famine/time of hunger/starvation
   d) adventure **(4 marks)**

Pages 26–27
Challenge 1
1. a) informal   b) formal
   c) informal   d) formal **(4 marks)**
Challenge 2
1. a) Hello, we are going to have a good time (or fun) at the beach.
   b) You had better pack or you will be late.
   c) He did not want to leave the meeting, as he had not spoken yet.
   d) "Where is the treasure map, Captain?" **(4 marks)**
Challenge 3
1. a) no   b) yes
   c) Chat with parents
   d) they are free, well balanced and nutritious
   e) formal   f) informal **(6 marks)**

Pages 28–29
Challenge 1
1. a) My father fought in the Second World War.
   b) His unit ended up in Holland.
   c) He bought a Dutch dinner service.
   d) His fiancée lived in Scotland.
   e) He wrapped the dinner plates in 1) straw 2) stuffing. **(4 marks)**
Challenge 2
1. a) Who? – The Ghost of Jacob Marley.
   b) What? – He visited his old friend Scrooge.
   c) Where? – his house, the bedroom
   d) When? – midnight
   e) Why? – to warn Scrooge about his miserly way of living **(5 marks)**
Challenge 3
1. a) informal   b) first person
   c) past tense   d) happy
   e) To show how much the writer likes chocolate pudding. **(5 marks)**

Pages 30–31
Challenge 1
1. acrostic – A poem with a word written vertically and each line of the poem beginning with a letter of the word.
haiku – A three-line poem with each line having a set number of syllables. It originated in Japan.
limerick – A humorous poem of five lines with a special rhyming pattern.
nonsense – A poem that makes no sense but can sound interesting or amusing.
non-rhyming – A poem without a regular rhyming pattern or regular verses which can use ideas in any order. **(5 marks)**
Challenge 2
1. a) limerick   b) non-rhyming
   c) haiku **(3 marks)**

Answers

Challenge 3
1. a) the last two lines and *Forward, the Light Brigade!*
    b) the guns   c) no
    d) 'Theirs but to do and die'
    e) 'Someone had blundered'   **(5 marks)**

Pages 32–33
Challenge 1
1. a) Alliteration   b) metaphor
    c) Onomatopoeia   d) simile   **(4 marks)**
Challenge 2
1. a) alliteration   b) simile
    c) metaphor   d) onomatopoeia   **(4 marks)**

Challenge 3
1. a) the seven ages of man
    b) the world
    c) mewling and puking
    d) no
    e) creeping like snail,
    f) The three dots are an ellipsis which indicates that part of the text has been left out.   **(7 marks)**

Pages 34–35
Challenge 1
1. a) five   b) Into
    c) a Springer spaniel
    d) He thought he was mad as the lake was very cold.
    e) Malia worried about Into getting cold.
    f) opinion   **(6 marks)**
Challenge 2
1. a) opinion   b) fact
    c) opinion   d) fact   **(4 marks)**

Challenge 3
1. a) He had a cheerful voice.
    b) He says "Bah!" "Humbug!"
    c) He felt happy, exhilarated, cheerful.
    d) Scrooge thought his nephew was poor and so could not be cheerful.   **(4 marks)**

Pages 36–37
Challenge 1
1. a) impersonal   b) personal
    c) A   d) inform   **(4 marks)**

Challenge 2
1. a) dinosaur   b) old
    c) A: There was a certain island in the sea
       B: I live in a world of coniferous forests, groves of cycads and fern-like plants.   **(4 marks)**

Challenge 3
1. a) news story
    b) Dan Smith, aged 22
    c) in Cowplain
    d) earlier today
    e) A man collapsed.   **(5 marks)**

Pages 38–39
Challenge 1
1. a) Sunshine Holidays 4 You!
    b) beach holidays
    c) summer sunshine, sand and sea
    d) where the best places are for your family   **(4 marks)**

Challenge 2
1. a) ten years old   b) it is more formal
    c) She begins by telling what she can remember.
    d) recount writing   **(4 marks)**
Challenge 3
1. a) recounting   b) reporting
    c) persuasive   d) descriptive
    e) recounting   **(5 marks)**

Pages 40–43
Progress Test 1
1. a) armful   b) happiest
    c) report   d) merciful
    e) tricycles   **(5 marks)**
2. a) highlight   b) flowchart
    c) landscape   d) database
    e) kilometre   **(5 marks)**
3. reading; interrupted; notice; disappeared; reading; unruffled; praised.   **(7 marks)**
4. a) crafty – devious
    b) almost – nearly
    c) hunger – starvation
    d) imitate – mimic
    e) vain – proud   **(5 marks)**
5. a) hero   b) rough
    c) repair   d) destroy
    e) liquid   **(5 marks)**
6. a) the crag   b) bright blue
    c) elephants   d) pit ponies

e) facts   f) wrinkled
g) And like a thunderbolt he falls.
h) opinion   **(8 marks)**
7. a) formal   b) informal
   c) formal   d) informal
   e) informal   f) formal   **(6 marks)**
8. a) persuasive   b) reporting
   c) recounting   d) descriptive   **(4 marks)**

Pages 44–45
Challenge 1
1. a) infrequently   b) antidote
   c) immobile   d) illegible
   e) irreplaceable   f) nonbeliever   **(6 marks)**
2. auto – self   circ – round
   tele – far   trans – across
   mis – wrong   bi – two   **(6 marks)**
Challenge 2
1. a) infrequent   b) bicycles
   c) anticlockwise   d) telescope
   e) transatlantic   **(5 marks)**
Challenge 3
1. unable; disappointed; forward; defrosted; recovered; irreplaceable   **(6 marks)**

Pages 46–47
Challenge 1
1. a) worried   b) observant
   c) assistant (*or* assistance)
   d) referred   **(4 marks)**
Challenge 2
1. able – capable of being – excitable
age – action – manage
fy – make or become – magnify
ful – full of – thankful
scribe – to write – prescribe   **(10 marks)**
Challenge 3
1. a) decoration   b) sunned
   c) travelling   d) possibly
   e) Caring   **(5 marks)**

Pages 48–49
Challenge 1
1. a) aisle   b) allowed
   c) alter   d) cereal
   e) herd   **(5 marks)**
Challenge 2
1. presents; sight; practising; missed; picture; piece   **(6 marks)**

2. a) loot   b) currant
   c) waive   d) mayor   **(4 marks)**
Challenge 3
1. fair – fare   ewe – you
   pail – pale   sun – son
   their – there   **(5 marks)**
2. a) ewe   b) Their
   c) fair   d) pale
   e) son   **(5 marks)**

Pages 50–51
Challenge 1
1. a) stake   b) flour
   c) waste   d) stare
   e) board   **(5 marks)**
Challenge 2
1. a) bazaar; bizarre   b) band; banned
   c) steal; steel   d) be; bee
   e) floor; flaw   **(5 marks)**
Challenge 3
1. a) father; farther   b) caught; court
   c) pause; paws   d) guest; guessed
   e) which; witch   **(10 marks)**

Pages 52–53
Challenge 1
1. a) accommodate   b) beginning
   c) cemetery   d) disastrous
   e) equipment   f) foreign
   g) guarantee   h) immediate
   i) mischievous   j) neighbour   **(10 marks)**
Challenge 2
1. a) occasionally   b) parliament
   c) queue   d) recommend
   e) separate   f) stomach   **(6 marks)**
Challenge 3
a) I have a spelling checker,
b) It came with my PC.
c) It plainly marks for my review
d) Mistakes I cannot see.
e) I strike the keys and type a word
f) And wait for it to say
g) Whether I am right or wrong
h) It tells me straight away.
i) I ran this poem through it,
j) You're surely glad to know,
k) It's very polished in its way
l) My checker told me so.   **(12 marks)**

Answers

Pages 54–55
Challenge 1
1. a) example b) worker's
   c) Ben's d) teacher's
   e) Lola's f) Fred's **(5 marks)**
Challenge 2
1. a) example b) birds'
   c) lawyers' d) cats'
   e) girls' f) blackbirds' **(5 marks)**
Challenge 3
1. Jake's; Hatch's; boys'; cleaner's; team's; girls';
   minutes' **(7 marks)**

Pages 56–57
Challenge 1
1. a) k̲nee b) plum̲b̲er
   c) i̲sland d) lam̲b̲
   e) solem̲n̲ **(5 marks)**
Challenge 2
1. a) knowledge b) Thumb
   c) scissors d) Wednesday
   e) wracked f) gnawed
   g) answer h) knife
   i) Listen j) write **(10 marks)**
Challenge 3
1. balle̲t̲; cor̲p̲s̲; balle̲t̲; throug̲h̲; nig̲h̲t̲; ex̲h̲austed
   (6 marks)

2. a) gnome b) climb
   c) gnashed d) chaos
   e) wreck **(5 marks)**

Pages 58–59
Challenge 1
1. a) there b) You're
   c) two; to; too d) Where; were
   e) their f) they're; their
   (10 marks)
Challenge 2
1. a) mischief b) diesel
   c) soldier d) sincerely
   e) surprise **(5 marks)**
2. a) accommodate b) strategy
   c) mischievous d) temperature
   e) guarantee **(5 marks)**
Challenge 3
1. a) desperate b) symbol
   c) rhythm d) secretary
   e) occupy; friends **(6 marks)**

Pages 60–61
Challenge 1
1. a) accommodate b) accompany
   c) accord d) committee
   e) communicate f) community
   (6 marks)
Challenge 2
1. a) 881 b) 286
   c) 98 d) jam
   e) yes **(5 marks)**
Challenge 3
1. lean: a) 1 b) 4 c) 2 d) 3
2. profile: a) 2 b) 1 **(6 marks)**

Pages 62–63
Challenge 1
1. a) take part b) alarm
   c) manner d) dismay
   e) frolic **(5 marks)**
Challenge 2
1. a) sunny b) dwelling
   c) weak d) persuade
   e) equip **(5 marks)**
Challenge 3
1. arm; battle; harmony; truce; grief **(5 marks)**

Pages 64–67
Progress Test 2
1. Sam loved reading stories on his tablet. He had
   returned from school and immediately found
   an exciting story on his tablet. He wanted to
   immerse himself in the story and imagine he
   was the hero.
   Sam had a brother and a sister that he helped
   to look after. His brother was five and his sister
   was three years old. They were calling him. He
   sighed, put down his tablet and went to see
   what they wanted.
   (5 marks)

2. a) Sam had returned from school.
   b) He wanted to imagine that he was the hero.
   c) Sam had a brother and sister. The brother
      was five and the sister was three years
      old. (3 marks)
   d) They were calling him.
   e) Sam sighed because he wanted to keep on
      reading the story on his tablet. **(7 marks)**

3. a) bisect (or insect; dissect)
   b) inside (or beside)
   c) impress (or depress; repress; compress)
   d) subway e) unsafe
   f) international g) misdeed (or indeed)

h) conscience i) foretell (*or* retell)
j) disagree k) transatlantic
l) inhale (*or* exhale) **(12 marks)**
4. a) mov**able** b) exist**ence**
c) assist**ant** d) major**ity**
e) price**less** f) sincer**ely**
g) horr**ify** h) moment**ous**
i) depend**able** j) observ**ant**
k) spec**ial** l) arg**ument**
  (12 marks)
5. a) I must write my letter of apology, it is the right action to take.
b) The fowl fell foul of the butcher and became his dinner.
c) When she went to wring out the washing, the woman took off her wedding ring.
d) The fur of the hare was soft, a bit like my hair.
e) The boy bought some scent for his sister which he sent to her for her birthday.
  (10 marks)
6. a) accommodate b) exaggerate
c) parliament d) suggest
e) soldier f) vehicle
g) temperature h) equipped **(8 marks)**
7. a) Leyla's mum was unhappy; she had lost the children's party invitations.
b) Jake's and Sofia's invitations were also missing.
c) The football teams' fans crowded into the stands to watch the match.
d) My team's kit was lost so they played in their tracksuits.
e) I'd like to hear her sing because she's got a good voice.
f) Let's go and ask our friends if they will join our team. **(9 marks)**

Pages 68–69
Challenge 1
1. a) young children
b) parents/carers
c) adults; older children
d) adults **(4 marks)**
Challenge 2
1. a) story b) letter
c) recount d) advert **(4 marks)**
Challenge 3
1. a) formal b) informal
c) informal d) formal
e) formal **(5 marks)**

2. Audience: wide audience
Writing: informal **(2 marks)**

Pages 70–71
Challenge 1
1. A observations carried out
B used his/her experience **(2 marks)**
Challenge 2
1. a) drowsy
b) they made the town look white
c) everything was hushed and quiet **(3 marks)**
Challenge 3
1. a) formal b) right
c) yes **(3 marks)**

Pages 72–73
Challenge 1
1. a) historical setting
b) background of character
c) description of place **(3 marks)**
Challenge 2
1. A describing a scene
B showing the reader a character
C beginning to tell a story **(3 marks)**
Challenge 3
1. Suitable answers such as:
a) ending b) beginning
c) beginning d) middle
e) middle f) beginning
g) middle h) ending
i) ending j) beginning
k) ending l) ending **(12 marks)**

Pages 74–75
Challenge 1
1. a) character b) writer **(2 marks)**
2. a) first b) third **(2 marks)**
Challenge 2
1. a) redheaded; green; brown
b) blonde; blue; pink
c) blear-eyed; hare-lipped; crooked
d) giant; grey; scarred
e) swift; small; neat **(15 marks)**
Challenge 3
1. a) scary
b) scientific
c) first person **(3 marks)**
2. a) end
b) beginning
c) middle **(3 marks)**

Answers

Pages 76–77
Challenge 1
1. The order of the points in each section does not matter so long as the correct points are included.
   a) **Introduction**
   Who is the writing for? (D)
   Set the scene. (C)
   Introduce main character. (F)
   First or third person? (J)
   b) **Development**
   What is the situation? (I)
   List points to include. (G)
   Develop the story as a narrative. (B)
   What do you want the readers to think about when they are reading? (E)
   c) **Conclusion**
   Draw the threads of the story together. (H)
   Explain how the story ends. (A) **(10 marks)**

Challenge 2
1. Further down the tree lived <u>Mrs</u> Lively, the squirrel. She could nearly always be seen hurrying <u>here</u> and there looking for provisions to put in her hiding places for winter wake ups. <u>She</u> was good at collecting nuts and seeds that fell from the trees in the clearing. She stored them for their winter <u>hibernation</u>. Her daughter helped her and looked after the dray. The <u>dray</u> looked messy as squirrels use lots of twigs to make their homes<u>.</u> They are not too fussed about how the outside looks so long as they are warm and comfortable inside and can sleep peacefully and safely when they <u>hibernate</u>. <u>The</u> squirrels lived in a dray that was tucked away in a sheltered nook in the branches of the oak tree. **(10 marks)**

Challenge 3
1. B; D; F; A; E; C
   The girl and boy were enjoying swimming in the lake. The sun shone and the wind whispered gently through the trees. The children were looking at the fish swimming below them when suddenly they saw a large shadow emerge from behind a rock. It was the ancient pike – a large and dangerous predator! The children did not stop to think. They swam to the shore as quickly as they could manage.
   "That was close," gasped the girl. "If the ancient pike had caught up with us he might have grabbed our net and taken our supper!"
   (6 marks)

Pages 78–79
Challenge 1
1. because; In particular; as; In the same way; so that **(5 marks)**
Challenge 2
1. Second paragraph: I remember when War was declared and Joe was called up.
   a) Any four: and; so; and; as; when
   b) 1936 **(6 marks)**
Challenge 3
1. a) ✓ c) ✓ d) ✓ g) ✓ **(4 marks)**

Pages 80–81
Challenge 1
1. a) The Mole had been working very hard.
   b) He had dust in his throat, an aching back and weary arms.
   c) It was Spring.
   d) How the Mole was cleaning and what equipment he was using to do the cleaning.
   e) Spring was moving in the air above and the earth below. **(5 marks)**
Challenge 2
1. Joseph was <u>twenty five years old</u> when he <u>became a soldier</u>. He looked very handsome in his uniform and <u>his widowed mother was proud of him</u>. In <u>1914 he went</u> <u>to war</u>. <u>He knew the horrors of the trenches</u> and learned that war was horrific. His <u>letters home</u> were always <u>cheerful</u> as he did not want to worry his mother.
   He <u>fought in the Battle of the Somme</u> and survived but <u>lost a leg</u> in the battle. He was <u>sent home to recover</u> and to the delight of his mother played no further part in the war. The <u>war ended in 1918</u> and Joseph had lost many dear friends. He thought war <u>a terrible thing</u> and did not want <u>his sons or grandsons</u> to ever have to go through <u>such suffering</u>. **(8 marks)**
Challenge 3
1. Order of sentences: C; H; G; I; F; B; D; E; A **(9 marks)**

Pages 82– 83
Challenge 1
1. <u>Helo</u>, you might be wondering who I am or what I am. Let me tell you. I am a <u>dinorsaur</u>! I live in a world that is very <u>diferent</u> to yours. You might recognise some of the plants that I see every day but many would be strange to you. I live in a world of <u>coniferos</u> forests, groves of cycads and fern-like plants.

Flowering plants like magnolia, holly, ginkgo, dogwood, horsetails and ferns make my world beautiful.

Dinosaurs like me can be found in the areas you now call North America and Euurope. There are large freswater lakes where England and the South of France will be. I live in the Cretaceous period and dinosaurs are large pant eaters or meat eaters. I am a herbivore which means that I am a plant-eating dinosaur. My herd name is Triceraatops. I have a short, strong neck that makes it eesy for me to pull at, and eat tough vegetation. I have three horns that I can figt with and I live in a herd that roams the countryside. We get to know the land and find out where there are good places to visit and where the eating is good.

a) Hello   b) dinosaur
c) different   d) coniferous
e) Europe   f) freshwater
g) plant   h) Triceratops
i) easy   j) fight   **(10 marks)**

Challenge 2
1. a) was   b) did
c) had left   d) had
e) was   **(5 marks)**

Challenge 3
1. Helen was a keen football player. She was a good member of the girls' team. I remember the first time I saw her play. She was the centre-forward and scored a brilliant goal. She will probably play for England one day! I will look forward to that day and make sure I go to watch the match.   **(15 marks)**

Pages 84–87
Progress Test 3
1. a) fire   b) sign
c) climb   d) right
e) friend   **(5 marks)**
2. a) young children   b) mixed audience
c) older children   d) young children
e) mixed audience   **(5 marks)**
3. a) informal   b) formal
c) persuasive   d) recounting
   (4 marks)
4. a) stampede   b) community
c) lightning   d) twelfth
e) Neighbours   **(5 marks)**
5. a) narrative (*or* autobiography)
b) autobiography

c) science fiction (*or* biography)
d) travel guide
e) feature article   **(5 marks)**
6. Order of sentences: B; C; E; F; G; A; D
   (7 marks)
7. a) to make greater
b) written or published list of events
c) a method or set method
d) dating from very long ago   **(4 marks)**
8. a) Windsor Castle is famous.
b) It was built as a wooden Motte by William the Conqueror.
c) In 1992 it was nearly destroyed by fire.
d) Over 100 rooms were devastated by the fire.
e) It was restored at no cost to the taxpayer.
   (5 marks)
9. a) requested   b) hoped
c) brave   d) abandoned **(4 marks)**

Pages 88–89
Challenge 1
1. a) ran – action
b) was – state of being
c) felt – mental state
d) were reading – action
e) roared – action   **(10 marks)**
Challenge 2
1. a) past   b) present
c) future   **(3 marks)**
2. a) are; were   b) was
c) Are   d) were
e) is   **(5 marks)**
Challenge 3
1. a) I will write my story.
b) I am cooking my tea and think I may eat it outside.
c) Hardeep played goalkeeper for the hockey team.
d) He will brew his mum a cup of tea.
e) The plane is late taking off for London.
   (5 marks)

Pages 90–91
Challenge 1
1. a) ringing; woke   b) Call; to sign
c) were; played   d) had been
e) thought; would   **(5 marks)**

Answers

Challenge 2

1.
a) are   b) realised
c) was   d) have
e) arrived   **(5 marks)**

Challenge 3

1. clasps; stands; watches; falls   **(4 marks)**
2. made; was; had; stunned; saw   **(5 marks)**

Pages 92–93
Challenge 1

1
a) example   b) slowly – how
c) hourly – when   d) frequently – when
e) roughly – how   f) always – when
    (10 marks)

Challenge 2

1. Yesterday; hard; carefully; slowly; quickly; carelessly
    (6 marks)

Challenge 3

1.
a) harder   b) good
c) smallest   d) further
e) most
f) The team tried harder after half time.
g) He was the most hopeful he had ever been when he opened his exam results.
h) She was the smallest of them, yet the most loved.
i) The children were the furthest from home any of them had ever been.
j) The team practised their game and soon they were the best team in the league.
    (10 marks)

Pages 94–95
Challenge 1

1.
a) must   b) couldn't
c) can   d) must
e) could   **(5 marks)**

Challenge 2

1.
a) can   b) mustn't
c) needn't   d) couldn't
e) could   **(5 marks)**

Challenge 3

1.
a) It must be a very good drive.
b) She can't have seen me.
c) It must be very cold outside.
d) We should wear name badges.
e) Shouldn't we always remember those who died?   **(5 marks)**

Pages 96–97
Challenge 1

1.
a) ran the relay race skilfully and swiftly.
b) was very happy when his family asked him to stay with them.
c) is built for racing.
d) can fill the heart with joy.
e) helped us to understand the culture of the country better.   **(5 marks)**

Challenge 2

1.
a) <u>The big boy</u> was wearing <u>his new trainers</u> on <u>the running track</u>.
b) <u>Sylvester the cat</u> chased <u>his enemy</u> around <u>the house</u>.
c) <u>All the animals</u> were hiding.
d) <u>The best defence</u> against sunburn is <u>strong lotion</u>.
e) Amelia likes galloping on <u>her horse</u>.
    (5 marks)

Challenge 3

1.
a) The unhappy girl/boy went to school with her/his friend.
b) The untidy boy/girl put his/her clothes away.
c) The ugly princess/prince married the attractive prince/princess.
d) The happy children ran to their mother for a hug.
e) My old tablet works better than this one does.   **(5 marks)**

Pages 98–99
Challenge 1

1.
a) The dog is panting because it is thirsty.
b) The children worked hard; meanwhile (*or* consequently), their teacher prepared a treat for them.
c) Noah wanted a dog; however his mum didn't want one.
d) I bought a big bag of logs from the market; consequently (*or* however) I could not carry it home because it was so heavy.
e) You need to have a bath; alternatively you can have a shower or a sauna.   **(5 marks)**

Challenge 2

1.
a) active   b) passive
c) active   d) passive
e) passive   **(5 marks)**

Challenge 3

1.
a) Granddad decorated the birthday cake.
b) The team used coloured balls for their hockey practice.
c) His dad had washed the windows.

d) Mrs Plumb, the vicar's wife, drank the tea.

e) The wind blew crisp packets and sweet wrappers around the square. **(5 marks)**

Pages 100–101
Challenge 1

1. **a)** I like the dog that lives next door.
   b) The young boy, whose football was found, is happy.
   c) I live in Manchester, where I go to school.
   d) The house that I live in has a garden, which is very large.
   e) Mr Smith has a daughter, who is a doctor. **(5 marks)**

Challenge 2

1. **a)** whose   **b)** where
   c) whom   **d)** who   **(4 marks)**

Challenge 3

1. **a)** who   **b)** that
   c) which   **d)** whose
   e) whom   **(5 marks)**

Pages 102–103
Challenge 1

1. **a)** I went to the shops and bought apples, oranges, bread and butter, but I forgot the milk, tea and sugar.
   b) The band leader walked to the front, took out his baton, and started to conduct the band.
   c) His dad was a happy, cheerful man.
   d) We wanted to go the beach, so we packed a picnic and left. **(4 marks)**

Challenge 2

1. **a)** Mr Smith, the butcher, parcelled up the meat we had ordered.
   b) The thief, who was sneaking around outside, decided not to break in after all.
   c) The children, who were all present, were excited about the visit to the zoo. **(3 marks)**

Challenge 3

1. **a)** 1,256   **b)** January 20th, 2015
   c) "Tomorrow, we will go back to school," Shanti said.
   d) In spring, the plants begin to grow again. **(4 marks)**

2. **a)** ✗   **b)** ✓
   c) ✓   **d)** ✗
   e) ✓   **(5 marks)**

Pages 104–105
Challenge 1

1. **a)** The teacher made them re-enter the room less noisily.
   b) The parents knew when their children misbehaved because they were all-seeing.
   c) Their son-in-law was a very tall man.
   d) The sailor told the story of the man-eating shark being seen in the bay.
   e) He designed an amazing T-shirt for the band to wear. **(5 marks)**

Challenge 2

1. **a)** The film was amazing – an excellent experience!
   b) How – how did you manage that?
   c) We found the children – they were very happy indeed.
   d) The pony – the second his owners had bought – got lost one day.
   e) My daughter-in-law has reworked her design for our living room – it's amazing! **(5 marks)**

Challenge 3

1. **a)** Mum's computer was green (bright green) with a bright green cover.
   b) They were going on holiday (for the first time) to Greece.
   c) Bert and Daisy were early (unlike yesterday), so the meal began on time.
   d) The boy's story (*My Adventures in Space*) was displayed in the school library.
   e) The poet Coleridge (he wrote *The Ancient Mariner*) lived in the Lake District. **(5 marks)**

Pages 106–107
Challenge 1

1. **a)** We are selling our house; we want someone to buy it soon.
   b) The lion survived the operation on its leg; however, it limped for a long time afterwards.
   c) Andy owned a cat, a dog, and a pony; he kept them in a specially-built wooden house.
   d) *The Long, Short and the Tall*; *The Incredibles*; *The Magic Faraway Tree* are all films I have seen.
   e) Marie, the taller of the two, was able to reach the shelf; we were all pleased as we could now have a biscuit. **(5 marks)**

Answers

Challenge 2

1. a) I wrote my shopping list: ten eggs, a kilo of sugar, a kilo of flour and some dried fruit.
    b) Please give the following information: your name, occupation, age.
    c) The flight leaves at 13:40 hours.
    d) The ballot results were announced: Ruth was the new team leader.
    e) To get there I had to run all day: the distance was daunting.
    f) You are going to read verses from *Macbeth* Scene 2 lines 1:6.
    g) I want to know everything: the date, time and place. **(7 marks)**

Challenge 3

1. a) For their sports day the children had the following:
    • egg and spoon races
    • hop, skip and jump
    • parents' races
    b) The holiday bungalow was lovely but it lacked a few basic items:
    • towels
    • blankets
    • washing powder
    c) The town was interesting for tourists but some things were best to leave out:
    • swimming in the lake
    • eating uncooked food
    • buying tourist souvenirs **(9 marks)**

Pages 108–111
Progress Test 4

1. The woman <u>was</u> standing on the deck of the boat. She <u>felt</u> the boat <u>turn</u> and suddenly she <u>was</u> in the sea <u>swimming</u> to shore. She <u>took</u> a deep breath. Then a strong hand <u>grabbed</u> her. She <u>was</u> <u>pulled</u> into a small rowing <u>boat</u>, she <u>was</u> <u>saved</u>! **(12 marks)**
2. a) present   b) past
    c) past   d) future
    e) present   **(5 marks)**
3. a) Robert was in charge of the computers; he had to mend them if they broke down.
    b) Mum thought the bird with a yellow beak was a blackbird.
    c) James was working hard to get the house clean.
    d) I am planning to go fishing tomorrow.
    e) Where is (*or* was) the box of chocolates?
                                   (5 marks)

4. a) My friends were singing beautifully in the choir.
    b) The monster walked slowly into the forest.
    c) He was looking for his favourite mushrooms, which grew prolifically in the forest.
    d) She jumped backwards off the diving board.
    e) The students worked hard but it was the student who worked hardest that won the prize.
                                   (5 marks)
5. Any suitable answers, e.g.
    a) We can have a curry for dinner today.
    b) Tomorrow we must have a walk in the park.
    c) Al couldn't reach the top shelf even though he was the tallest person in the shop.
    d) Could (*or* must; need) we go swimming tomorrow?
    e) You must (*or* need) not switch the television on as you need to do your homework.
                                   (5 marks)
6. <u>Years</u> ago, a family of mice lived in a hole in an oak tree. The oak tree was on the <u>edge</u> of a wood, near a field. An old hedge grew near the oak tree <u>and</u> formed the boundary of the field. The hedge provided shelter and food for the mice and they enjoyed living in their special place<u>.</u>
    The family <u>was</u> made up of a father<u>,</u> mother and four babies. <u>The</u> baby mice kept their parents busy, as they were curious <u>and</u> always looking for adventures and fun. The <u>hole</u> in the oak tree was a good place to live because it was so very <u>comfortable</u> and warm, especially in winter when the mice slept a lot.
                                   (10 marks)
7. a) <u>The ancient, dilapidated house</u> was creaking <u>in the wind</u>.
    b) <u>The sad child</u> was happy when <u>her mother</u> returned.
    c) <u>Some monkeys</u> were built for swinging through <u>the trees</u>.
    d) <u>Van Gogh's paintings</u> can inspire <u>the world</u>! **(4 marks)**
8. Jim was a smart, lively boy. He lived in a cottage with his mother, Mary. Jim liked helping his mother gather herbs, mushrooms and leaves for the cooking pot. Mary and Jim enjoyed making tasty meals together.
                                   (13 marks)

9. The football fans were excited – they were going to town! Alex, the leader, was organising the walk to the bus stop. The group had bought special T-shirts for the trip. Alex was amazed – such enthusiasm!

    They were on the bus; they would arrive in town soon. They had to be at the stadium by 14:20 if they were to see the start of the match. The fans were all keen footballers, so they said they would enjoy seeing the match.

    (8 marks)

10. Please display good manners in the pool:
    * no spitting
    * no bombing
    * no diving   **(3 marks)**

Progress Test Charts

Progress Test 1

Q	Topic	✓ or ✗	See Page
1	Adding Prefixes or Suffixes to Root Words		12, 14, 16
2	Root Words		18
3	Suffixes		14
4	Synonyms		20
5	Antonyms		22
6	Retrieving Information		34
7	Formal and Informal Writing		26
8	Comparing Texts		36

Progress Test 2

Q	Topic	✓ or ✗	See Page
1	Adding Prefixes or Suffixes to Root Words		12, 14, 16, 44, 46
2	Retrieving Information		34
3	Prefixes		12, 44
4	Suffixes		14, 46
5	Homophones		48
6	Common Misspellings		52
7	Possessive Apostrophes		54

Progress Test Charts

Progress Test 3

Q	Topic	✓ or ✗	See Page
1	Silent Letters		56
2	Audience and Purpose		68
3	Comparing Texts		36
4	One-off Spellings		58
5	Settings, Characters and Plot		72
6	Organising Your Writing		76
7	Using a Dictionary		60
8	Précis		80
9	Synonyms		20

Progress Test 4

Q	Topic	✓ or ✗	See Page
1	Verbs		88
2	Verbs		88
3	Verbs		88
4	Adverbs		92
5	Modal Verbs		94
6	Proofreading		82
7	Noun Phrases		96
8	Proofreading		82
9	Proofreading		82
10	Semicolons, Colons and Bullet Points		106

What am I doing well in? _____

_____

What do I need to improve? _____

_____

Notes